Penguin Education
Topics in history

A plague of Europeans
Westerners in Africa
since the fifteenth century

David Killingray

GW00455700

David Killingray attended two secondary schools, the
London School of Economics and the University of York.
He has taught in a number of schools in Britain and also
in Tanzania. In 1968—9 he was a member of the Schools
Council General Studies Project and produced a collection
of learning materials on Africa. At present he is a lecturer
in history at Goldsmiths' College, University of London. He
is married to Margaret Killingray who is the materials officer
of the Extra-Mural Division of the School of Oriental and
African Studies, University of London; they have two
daughters.

Topics in history

Alive and well
Medicine and public health
1830 to the present day
Norman Longmate

Foreign devils
Westerners in the Far East
The sixteenth century to the present day
Pat Barr

From workhouse to welfare
The development of the Welfare State
Ian Martin

Our daily bread
Food and standards of living
The fourteenth century to the present day
Richard Tames

A plague of Europeans

Westerners in Africa
since the fifteenth century

David Killingray

Penguin Education

Penguin Education, A Division of Penguin Books Ltd, Harmondsworth, Middlesex, England
Penguin Books Inc, 7110 Ambassador Road, Baltimore, Md 21207, USA
Penguin Books Australia Ltd, Ringwood, Victoria, Australia

First published 1973
Copyright © David Killingray, 1973
Designed by Arthur Lockwood

Set in Lumitype Century
Photoset in Malta by St Paul's Press Ltd
Made and printed in Great Britain by
Fletcher & Son Ltd, Norwich

Contents

Introduction

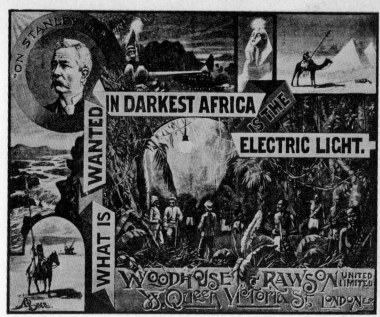

A late nineteenth century advertisement. Many Victorians had an overwhelming confidence in their racial superiority and also in the ability of their technology to transform the face of Africa.

Africa is a vast plateau of rolling grass uplands, great deserts, mountains and rain forests. It is a continent of tropical heat where snow-capped peaks straddle the equator and of semi-arid plains and sudden torrential monsoon storms.

The peoples of Africa, too, are as diverse. The term 'African' is commonly used as if they were one identifiable group, yet there are over 350 million people in Africa and many different ways of life: the Egyptian peasant tilling the fertile soil of the Nile valley; the Ghanaian farmer worrying over the international price of cocoa; long-robed Fulani from the ancient mud-walled city of Kano; tall, sparsely clad nomadic Maasai driving their long-horned cattle across the parched grasslands of Kenya and Tanzania; black and white workers in the mines of the South African Rand; and clerks hurrying to offices through the Lagos rush hour.

Although the way of life of most Africans would seem strange to us we all have similar basic needs and problems: eating, sleeping, working, getting married, having children, growing old, and learning to live with one another. People who live together in societies also have to cope with change. Many of the great changes in Africa over the last three hundred years have been precipitated by contact and conflict with Europeans.

The European explorers who cautiously sailed around the coast of Africa in the fifteenth century came into contact with Africans whose way of life they recognized as similar to their own. African beliefs and customs appeared strange to the whites but they did not necessarily conclude that black men were inferior. The king of Portugal happily addressed African rulers as 'most Christian Brother' in the same way as he did his fellow monarchs in Europe. However, the attitudes of white men rapidly changed. Europeans began to think they were superior beings to blacks whom they shipped in cruel conditions to America as slaves. And by the nineteenth century most white men regarded Africa as the 'dark continent', a mysterious and savage place inhabited by backward and superstitious people ripe for exploitation, evangelization and conquest. Foreign rule was, for most of the continent, a brief episode but it had far-reaching political and economic effects on many African societies.

In this book we look at some of the ways in which Africans have responded and reacted to these changes. In trying to understand these events we may, perhaps, not only learn something about Africa's past but also gain an insight into factors common to all human experience.

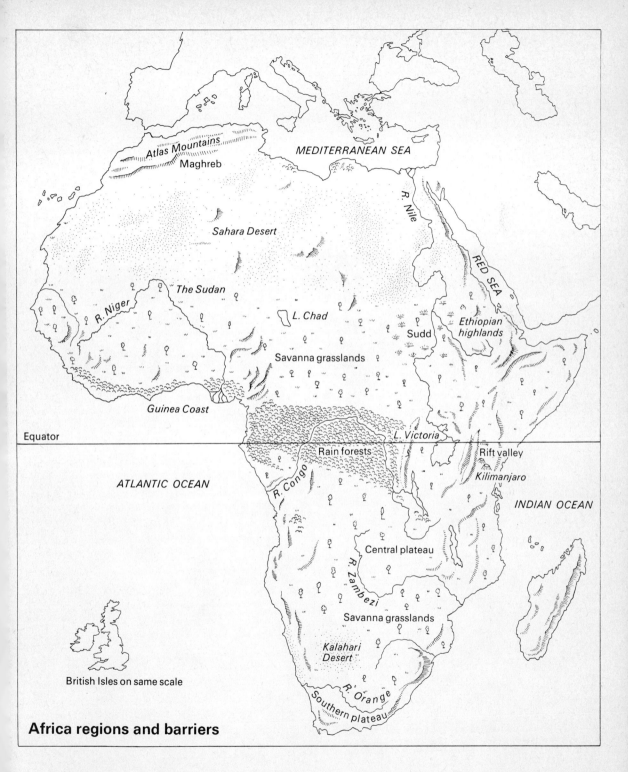

Atlas Mountains
Maghreb

MEDITERRANEAN SEA

R. Nile

Sahara Desert

RED SEA

The Sudan

R. Niger

L. Chad

Ethiopian highlands

Sudd

Savanna grasslands

Guinea Coast

Equator

L. Victoria

ATLANTIC OCEAN

Rain forests

Rift valley

Kilimanjaro

R. Congo

INDIAN OCEAN

Central plateau

R. Zambezi

Savanna grasslands

Kalahari Desert

British Isles on same scale

R. Orange

Southern plateau

Africa regions and barriers

1 Strange men and beasts

Rock painting, about 3500 B.C., at Tassili in the Sahara desert. Five thousand years ago the Sahara was much wetter than it is today. It was a green and fertile land and herders kept cattle and hunted wild animals.

Africa before the coming of the Europeans

Agriculture Early man in Africa depended for his food upon hunting and gathering. Agricultural techniques were introduced into Egypt from Asia between 6000 and 5000 B.C. although people in West Africa may have discovered independently how to cultivate crops. Many of the food crops used in modern Africa came from Asia and America. Bananas, yams and the coconut palm were brought by Indonesian sea-farers to eastern Africa 1500 to 2000 years ago; much later Europeans introduced maize, groundnut and cassava from America.

Iron Around 600 B.C. a knowledge of iron entered Africa and Europe from the Middle East. Iron-working skills spread slowly throughout Africa. From Kush, a great iron-producing kingdom on the middle Nile, techniques were passed to East and West Africa. With iron tools people were able to clear more land and grow more crops to support larger permanent populations; iron weapons gave a military superiority over people who had weapons of wood and stone.

Movements of people Agricultural and iron-making skills were carried through Africa by continuous small-scale movements of people. About 2000 years ago people who spoke the original Bantu language (known as proto-Bantu) moved from the Cameroons into the savanna lands of Central Africa before slowly dispersing throughout southern and eastern Africa. These movements continued until well into the nineteenth century and today Bantu languages are spoken by most people in the continent south of the equator.

Islam By the year 732 A.D., within one hundred years of the death of the prophet Muhammed, his followers had created an Islamic empire that reached from the Persian Gulf to the Pyrenees. The camel had been introduced into North Africa from Asia at the end of the Roman period, about 400 A.D., and the Sahara no longer presented an insurmountable barrier to the Muslim Arabs. By trade, missionary zeal and conquest they established the Muslim faith with its tradition of Arabic scholarship amongst the Negro people of the Western Sudan by the fifteenth century.

In eastern Africa Islam was carried by traders and settlers down the coast as far south as Mozambique. Despite repeated attempts Muslims failed to conquer Christian Ethiopia.

Kingdoms of the Western Sudan Little is known about the early Negro states of the Western Sudan. Ghana was at the height of its power in the eleventh century and controlled much of the gold trade across the Sahara to North Africa. In 1076 its capital was destroyed by wandering nomads, known as Almoravids from the north; the land was ravaged by war, trade was disrupted, and the weakened king-dom was eventually incorporated into the empire of Mali.

In the thirteenth century the Mali empire was created among the Manding speaking people of West Africa by a warrior called Sundiata, who conquered a vast territory on the upper Niger. Under two great Muslim kings, or *mansas*, Musa (d. 1327) and Sulaiman (d. 1360), Mali expanded in size and wealth by dominating the Saharan trade of gold, slaves and salt with the Mediterranean world. But by the fifteenth century, as Europeans were making their first contacts with the coast of West Africa, the empire of Mali was slowly breaking up, torn apart by internal dissension and foreign wars. As Mali declined Songhai, one of its vassal states, arose to take its place. Led by two remarkable leaders, Sonni Ali (d. 1492) and Askia Muham-med, Songhai extended its control over the middle Niger valley to reach the height of its power. Two of its major cities, Timbuktu and Jenne, developed as centres of learning known throughout the Muslim world and beyond. Askia died in 1528 and the empire was dis-rupted by struggles to seize the throne and revolution. In 1591 the bowman and cavalry of Songhai were overwhelmed by the firearms of a small force of invading Moroccans. Songhai collapsed and the Western Sudan descended into anarchy and disorder.

Europe and Africa in the Middle Ages

In the fourteenth and fifteenth centuries Europeans knew very little about tropical Africa. Two barriers isolated the continents from each other. The greatest barrier was the Sahara desert, a vast area of barren mountains and sandy wastes stretching right across North Africa from the Red Sea to the Atlantic Ocean. The other barrier to closer contact was the Muslim Arabs who controlled North Africa and who were constantly at war with the Christian states of Europe.

Europeans in the Middle Ages gained some of their ideas about Africa from the ancient Greeks and Romans whose writings they regarded as being almost equal in truth to the Bible. The Greeks were the great geographers of ancient times. They took an interest in the countries about the Mediterranean and although much of their geographical information was accurate some of it could be misleading. For example, Herodotus, who visited North Africa in the fifth century B.C., described a journey by 'certain young gentlemen into the desert places of Africa' where they were 'suddenly surprised and captured by a company of little dwarfs who took them, by a swift and violent river full of croco-diles, to a city where all the inhabitants were small and black and swarthy'.

The Romans had colonies in North Africa and they traded across the Sahara with the Africans of the Sudan. Pliny the Elder wrote about Africa in his *Natural History* but he mixed truth with curious myths and fantasies. His books, which were widely read and believed by Europeans in the fifteenth and sixteenth centuries, told of strange beasts and weird men living in a land of burning heat.

The descriptions of Africa that Ptolemy, a Greek living in Egypt in Roman times, put in his *Geography* also had a great influence on the way men in the Middle Ages thought about the continent. Ptolemy gave some correct information about East Africa but he also said that southern Africa was joined to Asia by a bridge of land. There were heated discussions by Europeans in the Middle Ages as to whether it was possible to sail around Africa (Herodotus claimed that the Phoenicians had done so) and it was only in 1498 when Vasco da Gama rounded the Cape of Good Hope and reached India by sea that the argument was settled.

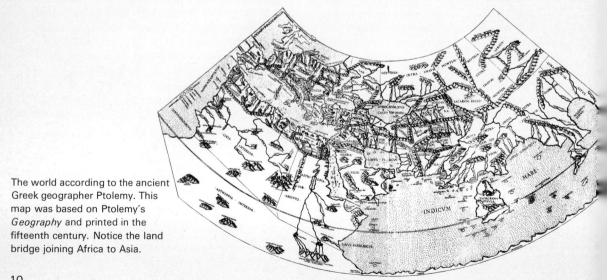

The world according to the ancient Greek geographer Ptolemy. This map was based on Ptolemy's *Geography* and printed in the fifteenth century. Notice the land bridge joining Africa to Asia.

10

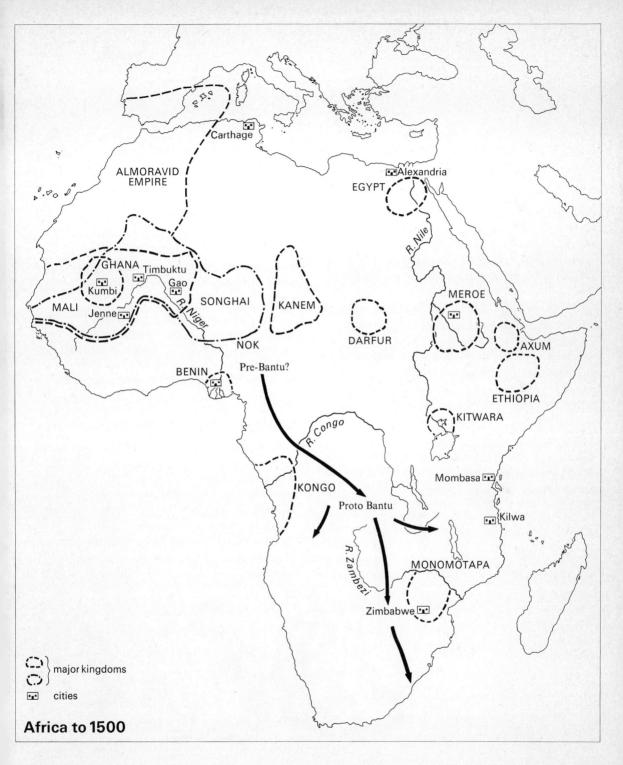

Carthage

ALMORAVID
EMPIRE

Alexandria

EGYPT

R. Nile

GHANA
Timbuktu
Kumbi
Gao
MALI
Jenne
SONGHAI
NOK
KANEM
DARFUR
MEROE
AXUM
ETHIOPIA

BENIN
Pre-Bantu?
KITWARA

R. Congo
Mombasa

KONGO
Proto Bantu
Kilwa

R. Zambezi
MONOMOTAPA

Zimbabwe

major kingdoms

cities

Africa to 1500

In the Middle Ages the few Europeans who could read Arabic learned more about Africa from the Muslim scholars who worked in Spain, Sicily and the Middle East. The writings of the great Arab travellers and geographers were slowly translated into European languages while merchants from Europe who traded with North Africa also heard stories about the African states of the Western Sudan from Arabs who regularly crossed the Sahara with camel caravans loaded with gold, rubies, ivory and slaves.

Travellers' tales about Africa were also popular in the Middle Ages. One of the most widely read was the *Travels of Sir John Mandeville*, a fictitious account that first appeared in the fourteenth century. It was full of stories about wild and strange animals, oddly shaped men, rivers of precious stones and marvellous kingdoms.

The whole of Africa is called Maritania and the folk of that country be black and they be called Moors. In that part is a well that in the day is so hot that no man may drink from it, and in the night it is so cold that no man may put his hand therein. In that country be folk that have but one foot and they go so blue that it is marvellous. And the foot is so large that it shadoweth all the body against the sun when they lie down to rest. In a certain island to the south live folk of strange build that have no heads, and their eyes be in their shoulders. And their mouth is crooked as a horseshoe, and that is in the midst of their breast. And in another isle be folk that have the face all flat, all plain without nose and without mouth, but they have two small holes all round instead of their eyes, and their mouth is flat also without lips.

Somewhere in Africa, so another popular tale went, lived a powerful Christian king known as Prester John, or John the Priest, who ruled in a splendour of wealth and might 'surpassing in virtue, riches and power all creation under heaven'. A sixteenth-century Italian poem proclaimed:

In Aethiopia's realm Senapus reigns,
Whose sceptre is the cross; of cities brave,
Of men, of gold possessed, and broad domains,
Which the Red Sea's extremest waters lave.
A faith well nigh like ours that king maintains,
Which man from his primeval doom may save.
Here, save I err in what their rites require,
The swarthy people are baptized with fire.

European knowledge about Africa increased in the sixteenth century as the coastline of the continent was explored and with the publication of Leo Africanus's *History and Description of Africa*. Leo was a Moor from Spain who travelled to the kingdoms of the Western Sudan as a diplomat. In 1518 he was captured by pirates in the Mediterranean and sold as a slave in Italy. He came to the notice of Pope Leo X who freed him. His *History* was written in Italian

Fabulous creatures from the Nuremberg Chronicle of 1493.

and it provided one of the first really accurate eye-witness accounts of the empires of the interior of West Africa. As such it remained one of the most valuable sources of information for explorers and geographers right up to the end of the eighteenth century. This description of Timbuktu is taken from the English edition of 1600.

Tombuto is situate within twelve miles of a certaine branch of Niger, all the houses whereof are now changed into cottages built of chalke, and covered with thatch. Howbeit there is a most stately temple to be seene, the wals thereof are made of stone and lime; and a princely palace also built by a most excellent workeman of Granada. Here are many shops of artificers, and merchants, and especially of such as weave linen and cotton cloth. And hither do the Barbaric-merchants bring cloth of Europe. . . . The inhabitants, and especially strangers there residing, are exceeding rich, insomuch that the King that now is married both his daughters unto two rich merchants. . . . Corne, cattle, milke and butter this region yeeldeth in great abundance: but salt is verie scarce here; for it is brought hither by land from Tegaza, which is five hundred miles distant. . . .

The rich King of Tombuto hath many plates and scepters of gold, some whereof weigh 1300 poundes: and he keepes a magnificent and well furnished court. . . . He hath alwaies three thousand hoursemen, and a great number of footmen that shoot poysoned arrowes, attending upon him. They have often skirmishes with those that refuse to pay tribute, and so many as they take, they sell unto the merchants of Tombuto. . . . Here are great store of doctors, judges, priests, and other learned men, that are bountifully maintained at the King's cost and charges. And hither are brought divers manuscripts or written bookes out of Barbarie which are sold for more money than any other merchandize. The coine of Tombuto is of gold without any stampe or superscription; but in matters of small value they use certaine shels brought hither out of the Kingdome of Persia, fower hundred of which shels are worth a ducato. . . . The inhabitants are people of a gentle and cherefull disposition, and spend a great part of the night in singing and dancing through all the streets of the citie: they keep great store of men and women slaves, and their town is much in danger of fire: at my second being there half the town almost was burnt in five hours space. Without the suburbs there are no gardens or orchards at all.

Arabs in Africa

Arab travellers visited and described the African states of the Western Sudan long before Europeans knew much about the continent. In 1067 Abdullah Al Bekri, a Muslim from Granada in Spain, wrote about the power and religious tolerance of the king of Ghana:

'Ghana is the title of the kings of this people, while the name of their country is Wagadu. The king who governs them at present is called Tenkaminen and he is master of a large empire and a formidable power. The king of Ghana can put two hundred thousand warriors in the field, more than forty thousand being armed with bow and arrow.

Ghana is comprised of two towns situated in a plain. The one inhabited by Muslims is very large and includes twelve mosques in which the Friday prayers are celebrated. All these mosques have their *imams*, their *muezzins* and their paid readers. The town possesses legal experts and learned men. . . .

The town inhabited by the king is six miles from this, and bears the name of El Ghaba, "the forest, the wood". The land between them is covered with dwellings. The buildings are constructed of stone and acacia wood. The king's dwelling is made up of a castle and several huts with round roofs and all of them surrounded by a fencing like a wall. In the king's town, not far from the royal court of justice, is a mosque where the Muslims who come to carry out a mission with the prince go to pray. The king's town is surrounded by huts and clumps of trees and copses, in which dwell the magicians of the nation, entrusted with the religious cult; it is there that they have placed the idols and tombs of their sovereigns.

When the king gives audience to his people, to listen to their complaints and set them to rights, he sits in a pavilion around which stand ten pages holding shields and gold-mounted swords; and on his right hand are the sons of the princes of his

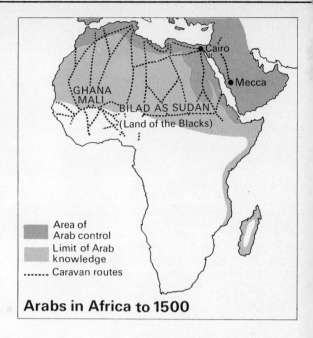

Arabs in Africa to 1500

Area of Arab control
Limit of Arab knowledge
.... Caravan routes

empire, splendidly clad and with gold plaited in their hair. . . .

All pieces of native gold found in the mines of the empire belong to the sovereign, although he lets the public have the gold dust that everybody knows about; without this precaution, gold would become so abundant as practically to lose its value. Certain Negroes from here are traders and carry gold dust all over the place.'

Muhammad ibn Battuta journeyed through Asia and Africa. He visited the kingdom of Mali in 1352, at that time ruled by the great king Sulaiman.

'Among the admirable qualities of these people, the following are to be noted:
1 The small number of acts of injustice that one finds there; for the Negroes are of all peoples those who most abhor injustice. The sultan pardons no one who is guilty of it.
2 The complete and general safety one enjoys throughout the land. The traveller has no more

reason than the man who stays at home to fear brigands, thieves or ravishers.

3 The blacks do not confiscate the goods of Arabs who die in their country, not even when these consist of big treasures. They deposit them, on the contrary, with a man of confidence among the Arabs until those who have a right to the goods present themselves and take possession.

4 They make their prayers punctually; they assiduously attend their meetings of the faithful, and punish their children if they should fail in this. On Fridays, anyone who is late at the mosque will find nowhere to pray, the crowd is so great.

5 The Negroes wear fine, newly washed white garments on Fridays for public prayers.

6 They zealously learn the Koran by heart. Those children who are neglectful in this are put in chains until they have memorized the Koran. On one festival day I visited the *qadi* and saw children thus enchained and asked him: ''Will you not let them free?'' He replied: ''Only when they know their Koran by heart.''

But these people have some deplorable customs, as for example:

1 Women servants, slave women and young girls go about quite naked, not even concealing their sexual parts. I saw many like this during Ramadhan.

2 Women go naked into the sultan's presence, too, without even a veil; his daughters also go about naked.

3 The blacks throw dust and cinders on their heads as a sign of good manners and respect.

4 They have buffoons who appear before the sultan when the poets are reciting their praise-songs.

5 And then a good number of Negroes eat the flesh of dogs and donkeys.'

Black slaves working an Arab ship. Many Arabs despised Africans. One famous Arab writer of the ninth century A.D. said: 'The Negroes are the worst of men and the most vicious creatures.'

Mansa Musa, Emperor of Mali on his throne, shown on the Catalan map drawn in Spain, 1375. Long before they explored the coast of West Africa, Europeans heard from Arabs about the Kingdoms of the Western Sudan.

2 White sails, war and corruption

Benin Bronze of a Portuguese soldier of the sixteenth century.

Europe and Africa from the fourteenth to the sixteenth century

1320 Mali at the height of its power and in control of the Saharan trade with the Mediterranean.

1415 Portuguese capture Ceuta in North Africa.

1441 First slaves brought by sea to Europe from West Africa.

1450 West African Kingdom of Mali declining. The Rozwi empire of Mwene Mutapa in Central Africa at its greatest height.

1460 Sonni Ali rapidly expanded Empire of Songhai in Western Sudan.

1480 Islam slowly spreading into Northern Nigeria and the Gambia. Revolt of the Changamire against Mwene Mutapa.

Portuguese baptizing in Kongo.

Portuguese priests and officials in West Africa.

1482 Portuguese built first European trading fort in West Africa at Elmina. They also established contact with Benin.

1490 King of Kongo invites Portuguese to send missionaries and craftsmen to his country.

1498 Africa circumnavigated by Vasco da Gama who opened a sea route to India.

1505 Kilwa captured by the Portuguese.

1506 Nzinga Mvemba comes to throne of Kongo and begins his attempts to modernize his state with Portuguese help.

1513 Start of trans-Atlantic slave trade.

1553 English traders visit Benin for the first time.

New animals: a sixteenth-century engraving of the Zebra.

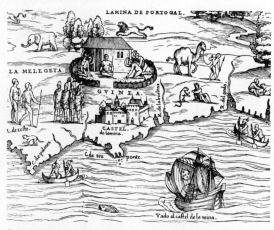

Fort at Elmina, 'The Mine', on the Gold Coast.

1571 Portuguese start conquest of Angola and send expeditions up the Zambezi valley into the country of Mwene Mutapa.

1591 Moroccan invasion of Western Sudan and collapse of Songhai Empire.

Nzinga Mvemba:
the modernist king of Kongo

One day the *Tukusunia Tungunga* [white men] arrived in ships with wings, which shone in the sun like knives. They fought hard battles with the Ngola and spat fire at him. They conquered his salt pans, and the Ngola fled inland. Some of his bolder subjects remained by the sea and when the white men came they exchanged eggs and chickens for cloth and beads. The white men came yet again. They brought us maize, cassava, knives and hoes, groundnuts and tobacco. From that time until our day the Whites brought us nothing more but wars and miseries.

> A story of the Pende people who lived
> on the coast of Angola in the fifteenth century

In the year 1506 a Kongolese Christian prince, with the help of the Portuguese, secured the throne of Kongo and in traditional manner killed his pagan brother and rival. Nzinga Mvemba, or Dom Afonso by his Christian name, ruled the Kongo for nearly forty years, at about the same time, and for almost as long, as Henry VIII in England.

Nzinga was a remarkable man. There was no clear law of succession to the throne of Kongo and the King, or *manikongo*, maintained a strong central authority only by his personality and ability. The kingdom had a population of two to three million people and stretched from the coast three hundred miles inland across grass lands to the forests, and south from the river Congo into the vassal country of the Mbundu. There were six provinces under governors whom the king ruled from his capital of Mbanza, the modern São Salvador. Nzinga was far-sighted in governing this large country and shrewd in his dealings with the Europeans. 'The king is the absolute lord of all the kingdom and there is no one who can say him nay,' wrote one Portuguese observer. Nzinga was educated by a priest and therefore he spoke and wrote Portuguese and Latin. And according to many rather uncritical ecclesiastics he was a devout Christian, being described by some as 'more angel than man',

as 'a model of the evangelical faith', and as 'the apostle of the Kongo'.

The Portuguese first arrived in Kongo in the 1480s. Within a few years the *mani* Nkuwu, the father of Nzinga, had been baptized and had welcomed Portuguese missionaries and craftsmen into his country. He saw great advantages in an alliance with such powerful foreigners while the Portuguese hoped that Kongo might adjoin the mythical kingdom of Prester John, and that both countries would be allies against Islam. With a baptized king Kongo was regarded by the Portuguese as an equal member of the community of Christian nations; Cameos, the great sixteenth-century Portuguese poet, described it in his *Lusiads* as 'the greatest of the kingdoms'. But to the *mani* Christianity was a cloak of convenience and despite the urgings of the missionaries he refused to give up his several wives, or to abandon the traditional religion of the Kongo.

Why Europeans went to Africa

'He desired to know what lay beyond the Canary Islands and Cape Bajador . . . to find countries from which gold came to Morocco across the Sahara in order to open profitable trade with them; to discover the extent of the powers of the Moors, to convert people to Christianity and to seek an alliance with any Christian prince who might be found; to engage in noble conquests and above all to attempt the discovery of things which were hidden from other men.'

Gomes Eanes de Zurara, the Portuguese chronicler, writing in 1483, on the motives of Henry the Navigator who encouraged the exploration of Africa.

When Nzinga became the *mani* the Kongo moved into a period of close cooperation with the Portuguese. Nzinga understood more clearly than had his father the political value of European cultural and technical skills in strengthening his authority over his people. He realized that education linked closely to Christianity would help promote this end. A recent writer has described him as 'a modernist king' who tried to bring his country into line with the Europe of the sixteenth century. In his attempts at modernization Nzinga had the sympathy and support of King Manuel of distant Portugal who addressed him as 'most Christian brother'. Nzinga asked for military help, for technicians, craftsmen, priests and schoolteachers, and these were sent by regular expeditions to the Kongo. Not all proved suitable. Some were rude to the Africans; others were idle, drunken or living with mistresses, and the *manikongo* had to ask Manuel to send a representative who would have control over Portuguese citizens in the Kongo. When the ambassador from Lisbon arrived in 1512 he brought with him a *regimento*, or instructions, from Manuel that suggested ways in which the Kongo could be Christianized and brought into closer cooperation with the Portuguese. Nzinga adopted some of the ideas in the *regimento* but when he read through the long and harsh Portuguese code of laws he jokingly asked, 'What is the penalty in Portugal for anyone who puts his feet on the ground?' He strengthened the nobility and had them change their traditional clothes of raffia cloth and animal skins for 'mantles, capes, overcoats of scarlet and silk, hats and caps, and Portuguese boots'. Later in the sixteenth century the nobles were given ranks and titles as dukes and counts in imitation of European courts.

Portuguese influence in Kongo increased; the ambassador acted as adviser to Nzinga and the priests controlled the young church and the new schools.

Portugal and Kongo 1483-1665

With the *regimento* came masons and carpenters. In Mbanza, a town of rectangular wood and mud huts separated by narrow streets and dominated by the royal palace surrounded with a wall of stakes tied with vines, they built modest and simple stone churches. One became the 'cathedral' of São Salvador and eventually gave its name to the capital. But perhaps the description of the royal city as the 'Kongo of the Bell', because of its many churches, is an enthusiastic exaggeration. Nzinga encouraged the Portuguese to open schools in Kongo. He saw the value of a literate class of people who would help to strengthen his weak control over the kingdom. He sent his own sons to Lisbon for their education, and one became a bishop in spite of opposition from some of the Vatican cardinals to a Negro holding such office. In 1516 it was reported that 'in the capital there are a thousand students who are not only learning to read and write but are also studying grammar and the humanities as well as the things of the faith'. Another writer describes a school surrounded by a high thorn hedge to prevent unwilling pupils from escaping. Most of those who received this European-style education were relations of the king and the sons of noblemen who were expected to be the future loyal administrators of the kingdom. The few conscientious priests and teachers were hampered by lack of support and money,

The Kongolese city of Loango in the
seventeenth century. The king's Palace is
on the top of the hill. Criminals are being
taken away, possibly as slaves, in the right
of the engraving.

but one of their great achievements was to produce the first known published work in a Bantu language, a Kakongo catechism printed in 1553.

The Portuguese, of course, had hopes of the Kongo other than spiritual conversions and modernization. As the *regimento* pointed out, aid to Nzinga cost money and the Portuguese suggested trade concessions in return. There was always the hope of mineral wealth, of gold, silver and copper, but more immediately of a monopoly over the trade in spices and slaves. There were few spices to be had in Kongo. The gifts of ivory and palm cloth sent by the *manikongo* to the king of Portugal in 1483 when the Europeans first arrived represented the wealth of the country. The Kongolese economy revolved around agriculture and some hunting. A variety of domestic animals were kept such as pigs, chickens and cattle, and crops of sorghum and millet were cultivated by women and slaves on land cleared by the iron axes and hoes of the menfolk. The oil palm provided oil for lighting and cooking, its sap became a potent wine, its fibres were woven into fine cloth, and the leaves were used for the roofs of the houses. All of this represented little of trade value to Europeans but there was an increasing demand for slaves for use in Portugal and on the sugar plantations of the island of São Tomé. Nzinga, who was eager to have the cloth and metal goods of Europe, agreed to this and prisoners-of-war and criminals began to be exported from the Kongo as slaves.

The uninhabited island of São Tomé in the Gulf of Guinea was settled by Portuguese in the 1480s. It was a convenient base for slaving and the traders and merchants on the island soon secured from the king of Portugal a monopoly over the trade of the whole coast. The close cooperation of King Manuel and Nzinga, and the new trade route between the Kongo port of Mpinda and Lisbon, threatened that monopoly. The São Tomé traders did all they could to disrupt relations

between the two states; they stole presents and hampered the interchange of royal representatives so that in the end Manuel decreed that all goods taken from the Kongo should only be carried in royal Portuguese ships. By this time the slave trade from Kongo had rapidly increased and most Portuguese in the kingdom, officials, missionaries, school teachers and craftsmen, were actively involved in the business, some of them in league with the traders of São Tomé. Their dominating interest was gain; even wages were paid in slaves. Many Kongolese, 'desirous of the wares and things of Portugal', were partners in the trade, ignored Nzinga's orders and threatened to undermine his political power and authority. In a series of letters to the King of Portugal in 1526, Nzinga wrote:

There are many traders in all corners of the country. They bring ruin to the country. Every day people are enslaved and kidnapped, even nobles, even members of the King's own family.

At first Nzinga threatened to expel from Kongo all whites except priests and teachers, but he retracted and instead introduced a system of inspection which attempted to confine the activities of the slavers to his capital and the port of Mpinda. This was partly successful and fewer Kongolese were enslaved, slaves now being brought from the territories outside the kingdom.

The Portuguese were not only greedy for slaves; they successfully prevented Nzinga from establishing contact with other European states, hoping to keep for themselves the gold and silver which they believed to be in Kongo. They had no wish to share the trade or the wealth of the country with anybody else. Gradually relations between the Portuguese and Kongo grew worse. In 1540 there was even an attempt by some Portuguese to shoot Nzinga while he was in church. As the historian Jan Vansina has recently written: 'The

dream of collaboration in equality could hardly have failed more dramatically.'

Why did Nzinga fail in his attempt to modernize the Kongo? He was trying to do something that was almost impossible; to change the culture of an economically isolated, illiterate and 'pagan' society into a modern Christian one. There were never enough missionaries and technicians to help in this, despite Nzinga's constant pleas, and those who did come were frequently unsuitable, incapable or died from disease. Slaves and gain became more attractive to the Europeans than the development and conversion of the country. And Kongo also became less important to the Portuguese as their empire expanded in Asia and America. King John, who succeeded Manuel to the throne in 1521, had little interest in the African kingdom and rarely bothered to reply to Nzinga's letters. When he did send any help it was usually too little and too late. Although Kongo remained nominally a Catholic country for well over a hundred years the custom of polygamy and fetishism never really ceased; Christianity in Kongo was largely superficial.

Within a few years of Nzinga's death the Kongo was split by lawlessness, civil war and an invasion from the east by fierce cannibals called the Jaga. The weakened country appealed to Europe for help and became in all but name a Portuguese protectorate. The Portuguese, urged on by the increasing demand for slaves, ignored the royal monopoly of the *mani-kongo* and opened direct trade with the southern vassal state of Angola. Not content with this the Portuguese in 1571 ordered 'that the kingdom of Angola be subjected and captured'. By the middle of the seventeenth century Kongo had begun to fall apart and there was open warfare with the Portuguese. The final decline of the kingdom can be dated from the Kongolese defeat at the battle of Ambuila in 1665. A hundred years after this little remained of the first Christian state of West Africa. But among the ruins people remembered the great Nzinga. In 1889 a catholic missionary in Congo wrote:

A Negro of the Congo knows the names of only three kings — that of the reigning monarch, that of his predecessor, and that of Dom Afonso I.

Portugal and Benin

The Portuguese also made contact with the West African kingdom of Benin in the late fifteenth century:

'John Afonso d'Aveiro came to Benin City for the second time in 1504. He advised Esigie, the *Oba*, or king, to become a Christian, and said that Christianity would make his country better. Esigie therefore sent Ohen-okun, a priest, with him, as an ambassador to the King of Portugal, asking him to send priests who would teach him and his people the faith. In reply the King of Portugal sent Roman Catholic missionaries and many rich presents, such as copper stools, coral beads and a big umbrella, with an entreaty that Esigie should embrace the faith. The King of Portugal also sent some Portuguese traders who established trading factories at Ughoton, the old port of Benin. They traded in ivory, Benin cloths, pepper and other commodities

Left: Bronze plaque of the Oba of Benin. Many of the fine sculptures of Benin were stolen by the invading British Army in 1897, and can be seen in the British Museum.

The Oba in procession from Benin city in the seventeenth century.

in the King of Portugal's interest. Owing to the
unhealthy state of the country their commerce soon
ceased. But John d'Aveiro with the other missionaries
remained in Benin to carry on the mission work,
and churches were built. The work of the mission
made progress and thousands of people were
baptized before the death of the great explorer
John d'Aveiro, who was buried with great lamentations
by the *Oba* and the Christians at Benin City.'
from Jacob Egharevba, *A short History of Benin*,
1934.

Below: Ivory mask worn on the waist by the Oba. *Right:*
Ivory casket carved in Benin in the sixteenth century,
possibly for holding salt and pepper. Portuguese officials
support the chamber. The lid is like a caravel, or sailing
ship, with a man holding a spy-glass in the crows-nest.

Fair city of Kilwa

East Africa at the coming of the Portuguese 1500

Just before dawn on 23 July 1505, the eve of St James, a trumpet sounded across the harbour of Kilwa. A little later, amid the booming of cannon, boatloads of Portuguese soldiers made for the shore, the standard of the Cross of Christ at their head. They landed and took up positions on two sides of the town, and then as the sun rose, made their attack. 'As we entered the narrow streets of Kilwa,' reported Dom Francisco d'Almeida the Portuguese leader, 'volleys of stones and arrows rained down on us from the tops of high houses and terraces so that we suffered great damage without being able to injure the enemy'. Stones and iron arrows were no match for the guns and armour of the Portuguese and soon 'the Moors were pressed so closely that some took to flight and others were compelled to retreat and surrender'. The royal palace was quickly captured and the Sultan fled through the palm groves away from his plundered island state to the safety of the mainland. In a morning the Portuguese had overthrown the power of one of the greatest and most successful of the Swahili trading cities of the East African coast.

For 1500 years before the arrival of the Portuguese the coast of East Africa had been a centre of trade. The north-east monsoon winds blowing across the Indian Ocean from November to March brought Arab and Indian *dhows* to the East African coast with trade goods such as glass, porcelain and cloth. In the months of May to October the monsoon winds from the south-east took the single-sailed vessels back to Asia with their cargoes of gold, ivory, cotton, hides, iron and slaves.

Between the fifth and the seventh centuries A.D. two groups of people came to East Africa. African farmers who spoke a Bantu language moved into the area from the interior of the continent, while at a later date, immigrants from southern Arabia settled along the coast and on the islands of Zanzibar and Pemba.

The Arabs established small independent towns and soon dominated the trade of the western Indian Ocean. They brought with them their Muslim faith with its belief in one god, *Allah*, and also the Arabic language and its literature. The Arabs called the Africans the Zanj, the 'black people':

They are a people of great size who know how to use iron and are subject to a powerful king called the Waklimi. Waklimi means supreme lord; they give this title to their sovereign because he has been chosen to govern them fairly. But once he becomes a tyrant and departs from the rule of justice, they put him to death and prevent his sons from coming to the throne.

Arabs and Africans intermarried and gradually a distinctive Swahili culture developed along the coast. The ordinary people probably spoke Swahili, a Bantu language, while the ruling classes and the traders used Arabic.

In the twelfth century a group of Swahili Muslims known as the 'Shirazi' moved southwards from the coast of what is now Somalia and settled on the islands of Kilwa and Mafia. According to the *Kilwa Chronicle*, written in Arabic about 1520, they bought Kilwa from the heathen Zanj with sufficient coloured cloth to encircle the island. There they established a town, dominated their nearest rivals, secured the trade of the coast, and made Kilwa a great power. The wealth of the city state was largely based on the control of the port of Sofala through which passed the gold trade of Moçambique and Zimbabwe. All the towns of the East African coast, and those beyond, sent traders to Sofala for the gold. A Portuguese visitor wrote:

They come in small vessels from Kilwa, Malindi and Mombasa, and in larger ships from India, bringing many coloured cotton cloths, and many small beads of grey, red and yellow. And these wares the Moors [Muslims] at Sofala paid for in gold at such a price that the merchants depart well pleased. The Moors of Sofala, who are black and tawny, then sell these wares to the heathen of the Kingdom of Monomotapa who come thither laden with gold to exchange for the said clothes without weighing it. The Moors also collect great stores of ivory and this they sell to India.

Kilwa, like other towns on the East African coast, traded not only with India but also with China. Early Chinese records tell of the land of Po-pa-li which was probably somewhere in eastern Africa. We do know that in the early twelfth century wealthy people in the Chinese city of Canton had Negro slaves, but there is little evidence of direct contact between China and Africa before the fourteenth century. Most trade before this time passed through the commercial towns of central south-east Asia. Archaeologists have provided abundant evidence of these early contacts by the discovery of coins, beads and porcelain of Chinese origin, not only on the coast, but also far in the interior of East Africa. Kilwa's relations with the people of the mainland were far from friendly. According to Ibn Battuta 'religious wars, or *jihads*, were waged against the pagan Zanj, frequent expeditions being made to the mainland to make slaves and take booty'. There was a small amount of trade with the Zanj but Kilwa's

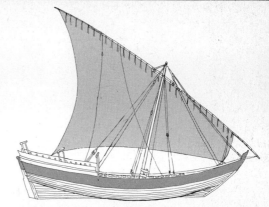

Sailing ships like this can still be seen today trading along the coast of East Africa. In 1498 the Portuguese explorer Vasco da Gama wrote that 'the vessels are of good size and decked. There are no nails and the planks are held together by cords. The sails are made of palm-matting.'

influence upon the people of the interior was almost negligible.

One day in 1331 a *dhow* carrying Muhammed Ibn Abdullah ibn Battuta, the great Arab traveller, anchored below the low cliffs of the island of Kilwa. The city was then at the height of its prosperity and Ibn Battuta, who had already visited Mogadishu and Mombasa besides many other countries, described it as 'one of the most beautiful and well-constructed towns in the world'. Above the crowded harbour stood the *Husuni Kubwa*, the great palace of the sultan, built on a site that gave it a fine view over the sea from which came cool breezes. Within the palace was a series of courtyards surrounded by cool rooms without windows, and with pieces of prized porcelain standing in niches in the plaster walls; the greatest luxury was the octagonal bathing pool which was filled with water carried by hand from the nearby wells. The town had about 10,000 black Swahili Muslim inhabitants of Afro—Arab origin, whom the Portuguese called Moors. The wealthy merchants lived in large houses built of coral rag stone. Some were two and three storeys high with flat roofs of stone slabs supported on poles cut from the nearby mangrove swamps. As Ibn Battuta walked through the streets he would have passed the finely decorated entrances to these houses with the

Left: First built in the twelfth century, the many-domed Great Mosque at Kilwa was one of the largest buildings on the East African coast. The ruins on Kilwa Island cover many acres and are still being excavated by archaeologists.

Right: The Fort or *Gereza*, at Kilwa. The Portuguese built the original fortress. Most of the present ruins date from 1800 when the Fort was rebuilt on the orders of the Sultan of Muscat, who had seized the town.

inscriptions in Arabic above the heavy wooden doors. Rooms were small and simply decorated with carved wooden friezes and carpets hung upon the whitewashed walls; in other rooms were stoves where rice and millet were cooked in three-horned pots over charcoal fires. Many houses had latrines cut in the stone with an adjoining wash basin. The poorer people, many of whom must have been darker-skinned slaves recently brought from the mainland, lived in houses of mud and sticks. They crewed the trading *dhows*, worked in the fruit gardens around the town, fished from small sailing boats, wove cloth from cotton, and cut and shaped stone for building. Ibn Battuta was impressed by the piety of the Sultan of Kilwa who gave a fifth of the proceeds of his raids on the mainland to charity, as demanded by the Koran. The Sultan minted his own copper coins and contributed towards the work of extending the stone-domed mosque with its many arches and pillars.

The arrival of Vasco da Gama off Moçambique in 1498 ended East Africa's isolation from Europe. The coming of the Portuguese also altered the whole political and economic structure of the forty or so commercial cities strung along the coast of East Africa from Mogadishu in the north to Sofala in the south. We get some idea of the bitterness with which these white foreigners were viewed by the Swahili from the description of them in the *Kilwa Chronicle*: 'The Portuguese were bringers of war and corruption — God curse them!'

Superior guns and ships helped the Portuguese dominate the Indian Ocean.

Kilwa had already begun to decline in influence by this time but it impressed the first Europeans to see it with its 'fine houses, terraces and minarets, palm trees and orchards that made the city look so beautiful'. In many ways it must have been very like plenty of small towns in Portugal or other parts of southern Europe with which the voyagers were familiar. Duarte Barbosa, a retired Portuguese trader, remembered the town many years after he had seen it in 1500:

There were many fair houses of stone and mortar, well arranged in streets. Around it were streams and orchards with many channels of sweet water. It had a Moorish King over it. Of the Moors there are some fair and some black. They were finely clad in many rich garments of gold and silk, and cotton, and the women as well; also with much gold and silver in chains and bracelets, which they wore on their legs and arms, and many jewelled earrings in their ears.

The Portuguese hated Islam and wanted to dominate the trade of the Indian Ocean. For this they needed bases on the East African coast; they also demanded the subjection of the Swahili states and regular payments from them. The coastal cities were isolated from each other and disunited and they were unable to withstand the superior ships and guns of the European fleets. 'The Sultan of Kilwa', wrote Barbosa, 'moved by arrogance refused to obey the king our lord and so his town was taken by force.' A puppet ruler was put in the place of the fled Sultan and the Portuguese built a fort on the edge of the shore to cow their new vassal state. The Portuguese captured other towns along the coast and exploited their rivalries with one another in order to weaken their commercial positions. Malindi allied itself with the Europeans against its wealthy neighbour, the off-shore island town of Mombasa, which also controlled part of the mainland. Mombasa was a powerful trading state and it fought the Portuguese for nearly a century before finally losing its independence in 1589.

With the Portuguese in control of the coast many of the trading states lost their purpose and they declined. Kilwa suffered but she was able to develop trade with the Africans of the interior who wished to buy foreign goods such as cloth and beads.

When the Portuguese empire of the Indian Ocean collapsed at the end of the seventeenth century the Swahili city states of the East African coast were weak shadows of their former glory.

Yalifa vumi makuni ya nde
kuwa mazibala yalisiriye

Stilled is the horn in the ante-rooms
for silence and darkness encloses all.

wrote a Swahili poet in 1815 of the once thriving town of Pate. And Kilwa never recovered, although it exported slaves to the French islands of the Indian Ocean in the eighteenth century. Today the splendour of the Kilwa that Ibn Battuta knew, and that Barbosa saw, lies in ruins on a little-visited part of the coast of Tanzania.

Zimbabwe

Across the rolling scrub and grass uplands of southern and central Africa are a number of stone buildings. These were built by Africans as royal courts and religious centres during the last thousand years. The most impressive ruins are at Great Zimbabwe, in Rhodesia, which were built between the eleventh and seventeenth centuries and became the capital of the powerful empire of Monomotapa. On the plain stands the great enclosure or 'temple', an elliptical wall thirty feet high made of rough-hewn stones without mortar and topped with a chevron pattern of rocks. Within the enclosure is a strange bottle-shaped tower of about the same height and nearby on a low rocky hill is a fortress-like structure cut through with deep narrow passages popularly known as the 'acropolis'.

The African builders of Monomotapa mined gold which they traded with the coast. For several hundred years Europeans believed that central Africa was the 'Land of Ophir' from where King Solomon took his gold, a myth that was popularized in the nineteenth century by novels such as Rider Haggard's *King Solomon's Mines*. When white men first saw Zimbabwe in ruins in the nineteenth century they refused to believe that Africans had 'the power and knowledge' to build in stone. In 1896 Rider Haggard wrote in a preface to a book about Zimbabwe:

'These buildings must have been constructed and the neighbouring gold mines worked by Phoenecians, or by some race intimately connected with them, and impregnated with their ideas of religion and architecture. Gain and slaves were the objects of the voyages of this crafty, heathen race, who were the English of the ancient world without the English honour, and at the ports of Eastern Africa they must have learned that in the interior gold and slaves were to be won in abundance. It would seem that this temptation of vast profit caused them to march inland. A mere trading expedition was impossible for they could not accomplish their visit to Ophir and return with the merchandise in a less time than three years. The working of the inland mines by the help of native labour must have necessitated the constant presence and supervision of large numbers of civilized men. It was therefore necessary that these adventurers sojourning in the midst of barbarous tribes should

Conical Tower, Zimbabwe. The purpose and date of the Tower still remain a mystery.

Plan of the great enclosure.

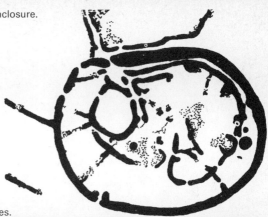

build themselves fortresses for their own protection, as it was natural that in their exile they should follow the rites and customs of their fathers.'

Even today some people continue to believe these myths rather than accept the abundant archaeological and other evidence which shows beyond all doubt that Zimbabwe was built by Africans.

The Great Enclosure, Zimbabwe, was a religious centre of the Mwari cult and was probably used for rain-making ceremonies.

3 The barbarous business

Slavery involves the domination and subjection of powerless people and continued well into the late nineteenth century as this photograph of an African slave boy shows.

Africa from the seventeenth to the eighteenth century

1620 Richard Jobson visited Gambia in search of 'The Golden Trade'. In the seventeenth century the Dutch, Danes, French and English competed for the trade of West Africa.

1629 The King of Monomotapa was forced to become a vassal of the Portuguese.

1650 The once great empires of the Western Sudan had declined:
'The Sudan was one of God's most favoured countries in prosperity and fertility. . . . Now all that has changed. . . . Security has given place to danger, prosperity to misery and calamity. . . . Disorder spreading and intensifying has become universal,' as-Sadi, the Timbuktu historian

1652 First Dutch settlers land in South Africa.

1665 Portuguese defeated the Kongolese army at the battle of Ambuila. Both sides fought under the banner of the Cross. Beginning of long period of weakness and anarchy in Kongo.

1688 Willem Bosman arrives at Elmina.

1700 Great increase in the slave trade during the eighteenth century; rise of an Atlantic economy involving the maritime and colonial powers of Europe. Rivalries of Europe extended to Africa. The Rozwi state of Changamire at its most powerful about the beginning of the eighteenth century.

1729 Africans drove the Portuguese from their East African coastal forts north of Moçambique.

1735 Dahomey gained an outlet to the Atlantic coast and became a major partner with European powers in the trans-Atlantic slave trade.

'The slaves are fastened together by the necks with a strong rope of twisted thongs, and then brought to the coast.'

1750 By a series of conquests the Asante Empire dominated the Akan states of the Gold Coast. Further to the west the Kingdom of Oyo extended its frontiers to control its neighbours, while the greatest state of Central Africa was the Lunda Empire which directed much of the trade to the coast.

1756 Olaudah Equiano shipped to the West Indies as a slave.

1770 First 'Kaffir War' between Dutch and southern Bantu-speaking peoples in South Africa.

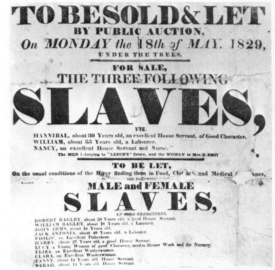

Slaves were private property to be bought and sold.

1772 James Bruce travelled to Ethiopia and reached the source of the White Nile. Slavery declared illegal in England by Chief Justice Mansfield. The decision was extended to the rest of the British Isles and by 1780 about 10,000 Negro slaves had been freed.

1787 Settlement of 'poor blacks' in Sierra Leone.

1788 African Association formed in Britain for scientific study of the continent.

1791 Successful slave revolt in West Indian island of Haiti led by Toussaint L'Ouverture.

1795 Mungo Park started on his first expedition to the Niger.

31

Afro-European relations to 1800

'Africa, this immense territory,' stated a popular English school book of the 1780s, 'is very little known; there is no traveller that has penetrated in to the interior parts, so that we are ignorant not only of the bounds but even the names of several inland countries.' This was not altogether correct, for a few bold men such as the Moorish traveller Leo Africanus had visited the Kingdoms of the Western Sudan in the sixteenth century, and the exciting accounts of James Bruce's exploits in Ethiopia were about to be published. However, European contact with Africa was largely confined to small trading posts along the coast and knowledge of the interior was slight. The only permanent European settlement in Africa was the small Dutch colony in South Africa. Most Africans knew nothing about Europe although pieces of information came second-hand along trade routes. Olaudah Equiano, the Ibo slave captured in 1756, said of the people in his village in southern Nigeria, that they had 'never heard of white men or of Europeans or of the sea'.

By 1700 a number of books had been written about the coastal areas of Africa. However, map makers continued to show the interior of the continent full of mythical objects, so that the poet Jonathan Swift commented:

S. Geographers in Afric-maps
With Savage Pictures fill their Gaps,
And o'er unhabitable Downs
Place Elephants for want of Towns.'

More accurate maps were produced in the eighteenth century. The Frenchman J. B. D'Anville, the greatest cartographer of his day, carefully checked the detail that he put on his famous map of Africa in 1727, while the Englishman James Rennell at the end of the century made maps that set new standards in accuracy. Myths about Africa died slowly. Prester John was no longer believed to be the priestly king of a jewel-bedecked fairyland but was identified as the Emperor of the remote and mountainous kingdom of Ethiopia. European knowledge of the great rivers of Africa had increased but their sources and exact courses remained unknown until well into the nineteenth century.

Except for the regions of Senegambia, Angola, the lower reaches of the Zambezi valley, and the Cape, Europeans barely penetrated more than twenty miles in from the coast. Why was this? The terrain and the climate of tropical Africa were barriers but not insurmountable ones. The rivers, which should have provided the easiest routes inland, were largely unnavigable because of frequent rapids and cataracts. In the north the Sahara, 'an arid desert of formidable extent', as James Rennell called it, was a great barrier, but caravans of camels had regularly crossed it for almost 1500 years. Although the forested regions along the West coast were thick they were not impassable and well-established African trade routes went through them. Perhaps one of the greatest barriers to European penetration was the popular European belief which saw Africa as a 'burning and savage territory'. Certainly the climate could sometimes be uncomfortable but rarely unbearable. A much more serious problem was what the Portuguese chronicler de Barros called 'the flaming sword of deadly fevers' — the malaria, yellow fever and dysentery that plagued tropical Africa. Despite a high death rate, estimated at between 25 and 75 per cent within the first year and 10 per cent each following year, many Europeans became acclimatized or threw off recurrent bouts of fever, and traders continued to come to West Africa.

The main reason why Europeans stayed on the coast was the lack of economic or political incentives to go far inland. Their principal commercial interest was slaves who were brought to the coastal trading forts by Africans. African states such as Dahomey

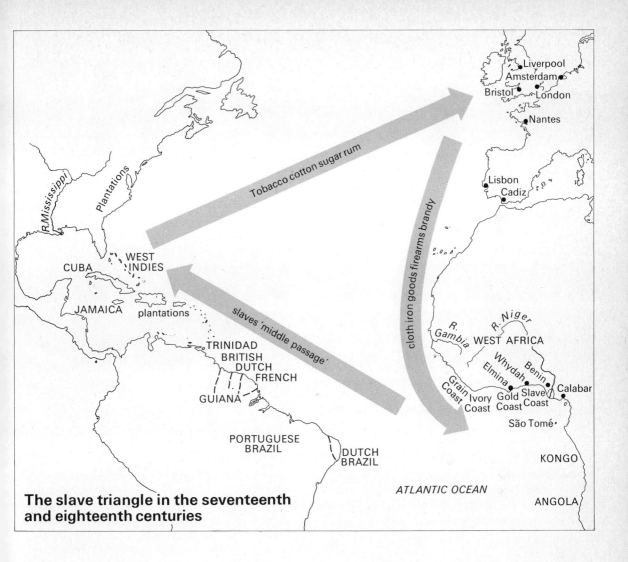

The slave triangle in the seventeenth and eighteenth centuries

and Asante controlled trade routes which they defended with powerful armies against rivals.

European trade with West Africa increased in the eighteenth century. Manufactured goods from Europe were exchanged for African slaves who were then shipped to America where they produced sugar, rum, molasses and rice for export to Europe. Over six million blacks were taken from West Africa in the eighteenth century, mainly by the British who dominated this triangular trade. As one writer of the time said: 'The Negroe-Trade is an inexhaustable fund of wealth to the British Nation.'

When the Portuguese arrived in West Africa in the fifteenth century they found states that were organized in ways similar to their own country. Many African kings were feudal rulers who governed through a hierarchy of nobles as in Europe. At first Africans were not regarded as an inferior race and their kings were respected as the equals of European kings. When the kings of Benin and Kongo embraced Christianity they were treated as members of the community of Christian nations. Ambassadors were exchanged with Lisbon and sent to Rome, and white and black monarchs addressed each other as brothers.

HERE
Lieth the Body of
SCIPIO AFRICANUS
Negro Servant to y Right
Honourable Charles William
Earl of S   d R
wh

I who was Born a *PAGAN* and a *SLAVE*
Now Sweetly Sleep a *CHRISTIAN* in my Grave
What tho' my hue was dark my *SAVIOR's* sight
Shall Change this darkness into radiant light
Such grace to me my Lord on earth has given
To recommend me to my Lord in heaven
Whose glorious second coming here I wait
With saints and Angels Him to celebrate

Where Christianity met Islam, as in North and East Africa, there was conflict. In 1505 the Portuguese burnt and destroyed the East African city of Mombasa. The ruler of the city wrote to the neighbouring king of Malindi:

May God protect you Sayyid Ali. I have to inform you that we have been visited by a mighty ruler who has brought fire and destruction amongst us. He raged in our town with such might and terror that no one, neither man nor woman, neither the old nor the young, nor even the children, however small, was spared to live. His wrath was to be escaped only by flight. Not only people, but even the birds in the heavens were killed and burnt. The stench from the corpses is so overpowering that I dare not enter the town, and I cannot begin to give you an idea of the immense amount of booty which they took from the town. Pray hearken to the news of these sad events, that you may yourself be spared.

Several centuries later Mungo Park recorded that the Muslim Mandingo 'look upon us as little better than a race of formidable but ignorant heathen'.

As the slave trade developed the relationship between Europe and Africa radically changed. European economic greed and a growing sense of superiority soon ended the early spirit of cooperation and friendship in West Africa. Europeans began to justify the slave trade by assuming the African to be a 'lesser breed'. By the seventeenth and eighteenth centuries most Europeans thought of Africans as inferior, and the biological, cultural and biblical ideas of the time all went to confirm this belief. Edward Long, the historian of Jamaica, writing in 1774, displays a not untypical prejudice. 'The Negro', he said, 'is brutish, ignorant, idle, crafty, treacherous, bloody, thievish, mistrustful and superstitious,' with hair like 'a bestial fleece', inferior 'faculties of mind', and with a 'bestial and fetid smell'. On the other hand some men who wished to criticize what they considered to be the artificialities of European civilization thought a primitive way of life to be a 'perfect image of pure nature', and a better way of living. The African was therefore romanticized in plays and novels as a 'noble savage', a well-known example being Man Friday in Daniel Defoe's *Robinson Crusoe*.

Thomas Day in his poem 'The Dying Negro', written in 1775, is enthusiastic about the black man:

In the wild wastes of Afric's sandy plain. . .
There too heav'n planted Man's majestic race
Bade Reason's sons with nobler titles rise
Lift high their brow sublime and scan the skies. . .
What though no rosy tints adorn their face,
No silken tresses shine with flowing grace
Yet of etheral temper are their souls
And in their veins the tide of honour rolls.

In the eighteenth century there were several thousand Negroes in Western Europe. A few were the

Grave of a black servant in the Churchyard at Henbury, Bristol. In the eighteenth century there were between ten and twenty thousand blacks in Britain.

Throughout Europe in the seventeenth and eighteenth centuries many wealthy people kept black servants. Black children were popular playthings. This is a painting of the Duchess of Portsmouth, the sister of Charles II of Britain.

protégés of European traders or the sons of African rulers sent to Europe for education. One such was Philip Quaque (1741–1816) who came to England from the Gold Coast as a young man, was ordained and returned as a missionary and teacher to Cape Coast Castle in 1766. The most distinguished African in the intellectual circles in Europe was Anto Wilhelm Amo (1701–c. 1760) who also came from the Gold Coast. He was an outstanding scholar and lectured at a number of German universities. Occasionally African diplomatic representatives came to the courts of northern Europe in pursuit of treaties. But most black men in Europe were slaves employed as flunkeys, personal servants or labourers.

In Britain after 1750 opposition to the slave trade grew. Largely due to the efforts of Granville Sharp it became illegal by 1778 to buy or sell slaves in the British Isles. And in the first decade of the nineteenth century a well-organized lobby had succeeded in getting Parliament to make the slave trade illegal for British subjects. In 1834 slavery itself was ended in British possessions. Humanitarians in Britain were concerned about the 'black poor', and they proposed a colonization scheme to return Negroes to West Africa. In 1787 the 'Province of Freedom' was founded on the Upper Guinea coast and became the basis for modern Sierra Leone. During the next sixty years Negroes from America and also freed slaves were added to its population.

The late eighteenth century in Europe was an age of scientific interest. There was an increased curiosity about the African continent — its geography, animal and plant life, and the customs of the people. In 1778 Sir Joseph Banks founded the African Association and began to seriously organize the exploration of the continent. It was hoped that trade would develop from this. The modern Christian missionary movement started in the 1790s.

Willem Bosman
b. 1672

'Gold was the principal for which we came,' wrote Richard Jobson about his trading expedition to West Africa in 1620. For several hundred years Europeans believed that 'no part of the world abounds with gold and silver in a greater degree than Africa'. Although he called his book *The Golden Trade* Jobson found little precious metal. Instead the Mandingo traders whom he met offered him slaves. 'I made answer,' Jobson wrote, 'that we were a people who did not buy and sell one another, or any that had our own shape.' Other Englishmen had fewer scruples, and Negroes had been bought, and fought for, by traders from England ever since the slaving expeditions of the swashbuckling John Hawkins fifty years before.

Among Europeans Jobson was an exception in being opposed to the slave trade. He said that Africans were 'made in the same likeness as Englishmen' but he also accepted the popular idea of the time that black men were inferior mortals. People argued about why the African was black; some said they had always been that colour while others said that it was due to the tropical soil or the sun's heat. Whatever the reason Richard Jobson, along with most other Europeans,

believed that Negroes were the descendants of Ham, the son of Noah, whom the book of Genesis said were cursed by God to be 'the servants of servants'. Men reasoned from this that blackness, and what they regarded as the primitive way of life of the Negro, was the result of sin; and observers like Jobson thought they saw, particularly in African sexual behaviour, clear evidence of this. Many Europeans therefore felt that there was nothing wrong in enslaving Africans and they believed it could be justified from the Bible.

In 1688 Willem Bosman, an adventurous Dutch boy of sixteen, arrived at the fort of Elmina on the west coast of Africa. He was employed by the Dutch West India Company and had come to learn the work of a trading agent, or factor. West Africa was a fever-ridden, unhealthy place for Europeans but Willem survived, possibly because sea winds kept Elmina free of malaria, and before he was thirty he had become one of the Company's most important officials. We know very little about Bosman. However, his chatty letters home to his uncle provide a mine of information about his work and acute observations about the people of the coast with whom he traded.

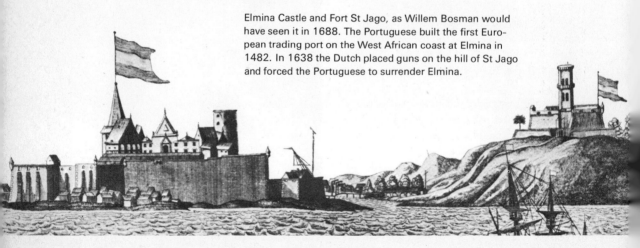

Elmina Castle and Fort St Jago, as Willem Bosman would have seen it in 1688. The Portuguese built the first European trading port on the West African coast at Elmina in 1482. In 1638 the Dutch placed guns on the hill of St Jago and forced the Portuguese to surrender Elmina.

A seventeenth-century Dutch Governor of Elmina. The black servant is holding a painting of the Fort. The stiff, heavy woollen clothing worn by many Europeans in West Africa must have been very hot and uncomfortable.

Christiansborg Castle. A grand 'Huddle of Buildings' constructed of stone by the Danes in the 1680s. It is now used as an official building by the Ghana Government.

Elmina overlooked the palm-lined Atlantic shore and was the first of the many trade forts built by Europeans along the Gold Coast. Originally it had been Portuguese but the Dutch had captured and held it since 1638. Some of these strongholds — and there was on average one every ten miles along stretches of the Gold Coast — were poorly defended, but Elmina was 'built square with very high walls, furnished with rain and fresh water sufficient for the use of the garrison and ships, and many heavy brass guns'. Beyond the walls of the fort lay the straggling mud and thatched huts of a once prosperous African town which, by Bosman's time, had been weakened by smallpox and wars. The Governor of Elmina lived in style, but for the seventy-strong garrison life was hard. Their living quarters were cramped and dingy and the roofs leaked; food was poor and fresh meat scarce. The officers and merchants ate large, long meals and, in an attempt to relieve the boredom of their isolation, drank too much.

Europeans rarely went inland from the coast. From their trade forts they competed with each other, sometimes violently, to secure business with African kings and middlemen who controlled the movement of trade goods to and from the coast. We can get some idea of the goods that interested Europeans from the names they gave to stretches of the West African coast: gold, which came to Elmina — 'The Mine' — from inland kingdoms such as Denkyira, ivory in decreasing quantities as the herds of elephant were hunted to extinction, slaves for the plantations of America, and Malagueta pepper known as 'grains of paradise'. There were also other goods such as hides, rice, mahogany and indigo. In exchange Europeans sold cotton cloth, rum, bar-iron and firearms. Selling guns and powder to Africans worried Bosman because, he said, it gave them 'a knife with which to cut our throats'. But, he added with a trader's philosophy, 'we are forced to it for if we didn't give them arms the English, Danes or

Germans would'. The lengthy and tiring bargaining over prices and quantities was usually carried out in Portuguese, French or English, for few white traders bothered to learn more than a limited amount of any African language. Much of the trade was by barter, although smooth, white cowrie shells, that were imported from the Indian Ocean, served as currency both on the coast and as far inland as Timbuktu. On the Slave Coast the cowries were threaded together, forty to a string, and in the early 1700s about 4000 shells were equivalent in value to a quarter-ounce of gold, or one English gold sovereign. Like many other European traders on the coast Bosman regarded his African trading partners as 'the greatest and most cunning thieves in the world', while for their part Africans who had been defrauded by Europeans saw treachery and deceit as part of the white man's character. Although very few African traders were able to read or write this didn't necessarily give the advantage to the literate white man, and Bosman marvelled that 'the Negroes are accurate in their trade accounts working out sums of several thousands in their heads without the assistance of pen or ink'. It was an age when Europeans had come to regard black men as inferior beings. Bosman was both more tolerant and more sensitive than most whites but he tended to look upon social customs and religious practices that he didn't understand as 'foolish and ridiculous'. He had a very poor opinion of the Africans around the fort at Elmina whom, he tells his uncles, compare well with what he has heard about the Russians:

The Negroes are all without exception crafty, villainous, fraudulent, and seldom to be trusted . . . they indeed seem to be born and bred villains. They are slothful and idle and reluctant to work, besides which they are incredibly careless and stupid. Negroes when young are far from handsome, and when old are only fit to fright children to their beds.

Bosman then goes on to use a familiar justification:

A display of the king's women put on for the benefit of a European visitor.

I don't want you to think I am prejudiced or hate Negroes but there is not a single person who has anything to do with them but also thinks they are not worth speaking to.

Although Bosman was frequently scathing about black men — as a patriotic Dutchman he also said similar things about his main trade rivals, the 'unhealthy and slovenly' English — he was careful not to offend the kings and merchants with whom he did business. Many of the rulers on the Gold Coast were powerful and only dealt with foreign companies when it suited them. They commanded armies, controlled the trade routes, canoes and supplies of food to the forts, and could divert their trade to rival Europeans. On a number of occasions, incensed by the arrogance and trickery of white men, African rulers captured their forts and took complete control of trade with the captains of visiting ships.

At Whydah, a small state on the Slave Coast, Bosman found the people 'industrious', and the merry and amiable king 'the most civil and generous Negro that I have met'. The king dressed in gowns of violet silk, or gold or silver linen, and lived in a compound of large mud huts guarded by four cannon and armed soldiers. The people of Whydah, including the noblemen, prostrated themselves all the time that they were in the king's presence, while European merchants gave up their swords and removed their hats before entering the royal 'palace'. White traders were treated with great hospitality, given huts in the royal enclosure and fed at the king's table. Bosman spent hours

Company marks on
slave branding irons.

Branding slaves.

gambling with the king who always paid when he lost but refused to collect any winnings from his Dutch companion. By respecting the king and treating with him fairly Bosman gained favour and thus trading advantages. The principal trade of Whydah was slaves. From the middle of the fifteenth century Negroes had been shipped by white men from West Africa, first to Europe, and then, after the discovery and settlement of America, across the Atlantic to the mines and plantations of the New World. As the slave trade increased, Africans began to play as active a part in it as Europeans. About a thousand slaves a month were brought to Whydah and sold to the English, French or Dutch forts where they awaited transfer to ships which stood about half a mile from the breaking surf of the dangerous shore. Most slaves were prisoners-of-war, criminals or debtors, although further along the Slave Coast at the wretchedly poor state of Coto, Bosman observed, 'their most advantageous trade, is taking a journey inland and stealing men, which they sell to the Europeans that come here in their ships.'

The first thing a factor had to do when he arrived at Whydah to buy slaves was to pay the king a tribute, or tax, in goods to the value of about one hundred pounds. He then had to buy the whole stock of the king's slaves at a fixed price 'which is commonly one-third or one-fourth higher than ordinary', and when this was done he was free to do business with other African merchants. In a letter home Bosman gives a vivid description of the way in which slaves were bought by the Dutch at Whydah, and loaded aboard ships for transport to their colonies in Brazil and the West Indies. They were brought from the prisons where they had been kept and examined by the surgeons who separated out the old, maimed and diseased:

The invalides and the maimed being thrown out the remainder are numbered and it is entered who delivered them. In the mean while a burning iron, with the arms or name of the Companies, lies in the fire with which our slaves are marked on the breast. This is done to distinguish them from the slaves of the English, French, or others and to prevent the Negroes exchanging them for worse at which they have a good hand. We take good care that they are not burned too hard, especially the women, who are more tender than the men. We are seldom detained long in the buying of slaves because their price is established, the women being one fourth or fifth part cheaper than the men. When we have agreed with the owners of the slaves we send them on board our ships at the first opportunity; before which their masters strip them of all they have on their backs so that they come aboard stark naked.

When the tide was right the slaves were taken out to the ships by canoe. Sometimes as many as four or six hundred slaves were put aboard a single vessel and there was always the danger of rebellion while they were being loaded. Bosman had trouble on only two occasions. In the first case he quelled the revolt by

The transatlantic slave trade

To most people in the seventeenth century the slave trade was just another form of commerce involving the chance of profit and the risk of loss. Captain Thomas Phillips wrote this account of the journey of the slaver Hannibal *from West Africa to the West Indies in 1693:*

'When our slaves are aboard we shackle the men two and two, while we lie in port, and in sight of their own country, for 'tis then they attempt to make their escape, and mutiny; to prevent which we always keep sentinels upon the hatchways, and have a chest full of small arms, ready loaded and prim'd, constantly lying at hand upon the quarter-deck, together with some granada shells; and two of our quarter-deck guns, pointing on the deck thence, and two more out of the steerage, and the door of which is always kept shut, and well barr'd.

They are fed twice a day, at ten in the morning, and four in the evening, which is the time they are aptest to mutiny, being all upon deck; therefore all that time, what of our men are not employed in distributing their food to them, and settling them stand to their arms. Their chief diet is call'd dabbadabb, being Indian corn ground as small as oat-meal, mix'd with water, and boiled well in a large copper furnace, till 'tis as thick as a pudding, about a peckful of which is allow'd to ten men, with a little salt, and palm oil to relish. Three days a week they have horse-beans boil'd for their dinner and supper; these beans the Negroes extremely love and desire, beating their breast eating them and crying Pram! Pram! which is Very good! They are indeed the best diet for them, having a binding quality, and consequently good to prevent the flux, which is the distemper that most affects them, and ruins our voyages by their deaths.

We often at sea in the evening would let the slaves come up into the sun to air themselves, and make them jump and dance for an hour or two to our bag-pipes, harp, and fiddle, by which exercise to preserve them in health; but notwithstanding all our endeavour, 'twas my hard fortune to have great sickness and mortality among them.

We spent in our passage from St Thomas to Barbadoes two months eleven days, from 25 August to 4 November following: in which time there happen'd much sickness and mortality among my poor men and Negroes, that of the first we buried fourteen, and of the last, 320 which was a great detriment to our voyage, the royal African company losing ten pounds by every slave that died, and the owners of the ship ten pounds ten shillings, being the freight agreed on to be paid them by the charter-party for every Negroe delivered alive ashore to the African company's agents at Barbadoes; whereby the loss in all amounted to near 6560 pounds sterling.'

shooting the ringleader through the head, and the other time, nearby English and French ships came to his help, but not before twenty valuable slaves had been killed in the fighting.

Without hesitation we would say that the slave trade was wicked, but few Europeans in the early eighteenth century thought so. They justified it with all manner of specious arguments: 'Negroes would be better cared for in America than in their own savage countries'; 'the enslavement of black men was supported in the Old Testament and not condemned in the New'; and the trade was the 'pillar of prosperity' of the economy of Europe and the American colonies. Bosman admitted that the 'trade seems barbarous', but he argued, 'since it is followed by mere necessity it must go on'. And when he was writing the trade in human beings from Africa to America was about to increase rapidly. In the following hundred and fifty years several million more blacks were to be shipped across the Atlantic in horrifying conditions before the trade was ended.

Olaudah Equiano
c. 1745–1801

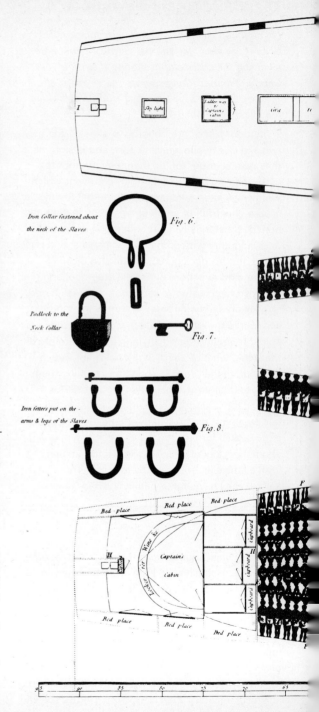

Among the millions of African slaves shipped across the Atlantic to America was Olaudah Equiano. He was only a boy of eleven at the time but the bewildering and terrifying experience of being crammed into the claustrophobic hold of the slave ship remained imprinted on his mind. Many years later he wrote:

The stench of the hold was intolerably loathsome. The closeness of the place and the heat of the climate, added to the number in the ship, which was so crowded that each had scarcely room to turn himself, almost suffocated us. The air became unfit to breathe and many of the slaves fell sick and died. Our wretched situation was aggravated by the heavy chains on our legs, the filth of the necessary tubs, and the shrieks of women and the groans of the dying.

A few months before this Equiano had been living happily with his large family, and a mother of whom he 'was so very fond', in an Ibo village amongst the tropical forest lands close to the River Niger. One day, while the house was unguarded, African slave dealers had climbed the wall of the compound and kidnapped him along with his sister. After several changes of owner — once he was bought for one hundred and seventy-two cowries — Equiano was carried to the coast where he was sold to a British merchant.

Many of the African slaves who arrived at the coast, strung together by ropes and chains, must have been as surprised by what they saw as was Equiano:

The sea and the slave ship filled me with astonishment which was soon converted into terror when I was carried aboard. I was immediately tossed up to see if I was sound by some of the crew, and I was now persuaded that I had gotten into a world of bad spirits. The sailors' complexions were so different from ours, and with their long hair and strange language I believed they were going to kill and eat me.

Long before Europeans arrived off the coast of Africa there was a flourishing slave trade from the states of the Western Sudan and from East Africa.

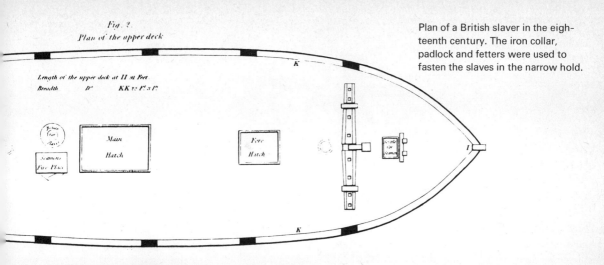

Plan of a British slaver in the eighteenth century. The iron collar,
padlock and fetters were used to
fasten the slaves in the narrow hold.

Fig. 2.
Plan of the upper deck

Length of the upper deck at II 91 Feet.
Breadth   D.º   KK 22 F.ᵗ 3 I.ᵗ

Main
Hatch

Fore
Hatch

Place
for Slaves

Seamens
Fire Place

Scale
for Seamen

K

K

I

Fig. 3.

D   D

PLAN OF THE WINGS, in the Men & Women's room, in
which the Slaves here described were found at the time of
the capture of the Vessel lying on a platform between the
upper and lower decks.
Breadth of the platforms in the Mens room DD 5 F.ᵗ 3 I.ᵗ
    D.º   D.º   Womens room GG 4 F.ᵗ 10 I.ᵗ

D

D

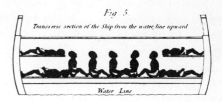

Fig. 5.
Transverse section of the Ship from the water line upward

Water Line

Fig. 4.
Plan of the lower deck

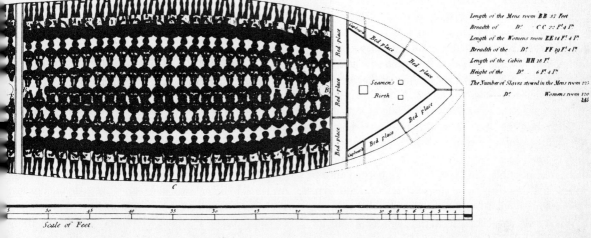

C

D

B

Bed place
Bed place
Captan
Bed place
Bed Place
Bed Place
Seamen's
Birth
Bed Place
Bed place
Captan
Bed place

C

Length of the Mens room BB 87 Feet
Breadth of   D.º   CC 22 F.ᵗ 4 I.ᵗ
Length of the Womens room EE 14 F.ᵗ 4 I.ᵗ
Breadth of the   D.º   FF 19 F.ᵗ 4 I.ᵗ
Length of the Cabin HH 18 F.ᵗ
Height of the   D.º   6 F.ᵗ 4 I.ᵗ
The Number of Slaves stowed in the Mens room 225
        D.º   Womens room 120
                                  345

5   50   45   40   35   30   25   20   15   10 9 8 7 6 5 4 3 2 1

Scale of Feet.

Neck band put on slaves who might attempt escape. The prongs were up to three feet long.

Under the most brutal conditions large numbers of blacks — and perhaps two out of every five died —were taken by Muslim merchants across the Sahara to the Mediteranean, and up the east coast by *dhow* to Arabia, and as far as India. The Koran prohibited the enslavement of Muslims and so raids were made on 'pagan' tribes for the women and young boys who were to become domestic slaves in the houses of the Middle East. There was a similar form of domestic slavery in southern Europe, but the Spanish and Portuguese settlers in newly discovered America wanted a different type of slave. They needed what were called 'prime slaves', healthy men and boys aged between twelve and thirty-five, who were strong enough to do the back-breaking work on plantations and in mines. American Indians and white convicts proved unsuitable to the harsh conditions and the colonists began to import sturdy African slaves across the Atlantic.

Starting in the early 1500s, and for the next four hundred years, competing European nations conducted a vast and brutal trade in human livestock. About ten million Africans were ripped from their homes and sent to the American colonies. Columns of black slaves were brought to the coast by African traders, sometimes over distances of several hundred miles.

At the European trading forts along the coast the slaves were exchanged for manufactured goods and then loaded aboard the ships. A normal voyage across the Atlantic, on what was called the 'middle passage', lasted seven or eight weeks, although the ship in which Equiano went took nearly twice as long and food became so short that the slaves 'were pressed by hunger'. According to John Newton, who had been a captain of a slaver, 'the object with our ships is to take as many blacks as possible, up to 250 blacks herded into a vessel that was little more than 100 tons'. Huddled in the stinking holds the slaves lay side by side 'with not as much room as a man in his coffin', as one captain put

it. Inevitably many slaves died, especially if the voyage was long. Many of the crew died as well, but few voyages failed to make a profit. Newton says that a quarter of the slaves died at sea but a recent estimate is that the figure for mortality in the eighteenth century was about 16 per cent.

One of the captains' greatest fears was that the slaves might seize the vessel. So the Negroes were shackled together, 'sentinels placed upon the hatchways', and guns ready-primed directed into the holds and onto the decks in case of revolt. When slaves came on deck for feeding and exercise nets were put along the bulwarks to prevent any of the valuable cargo jumping overboard. In his account Equiano records how two Africans 'chained together made through the netting and jumped into the sea preferring death to such a life of misery'.

When he reached America Equiano found that life as a slave was much more harsh than slavery in his own country. Black slaves in America were owned by white masters who regarded them as inferior beings, items of property that could be bought and sold, and worked like cattle. The slave had an economic value which depended on his use as a worker on the plantation, in the factory, or in the home. The slave code of Louisiana neatly summed up the black man's position:

The master may sell him, dispose of his person, his industry and his labour; he can do nothing, possess nothing, never acquire anything but what must belong to his master.

The system of slavery in Africa was very different. There slaves were usually captives-of-war, criminals, people who had got into debt, or those born into servitude, and their main value was as domestic servants and retainers who enhanced the social status of their owner. Though slaves were expected to do the hardest work they were looked on as humble members of their owner's family. Equiano wrote that among the Ibo:

Olaudah Equiano.

The slaves do no more work than other members of the community, even their masters; their food, clothing and lodging were nearly the same as theirs, and they were treated in a similar way to other members of the household. Some of these slaves even have slaves under them as their own property and for their own use.

In some African states slaves were trusted officials of the ruler and rose to high positions of authority. The 'throne slaves' of the king of Kayor were powerful royal advisers although they had to hang chains above their beds as a reminder of their servile position.

For some slaves in Africa life could be nasty and short. When a great man died in Calabar slaves were sacrificed at the funeral because it was believed that they would accompany him into the next world. Antera Duke, a Calabar slave dealer who kept a diary in pidgin English, recorded in July 1786:

About 4 o'clock in the morning King Ephraim died. Soon after we came up to look where to put him in the ground. About 5 o'clock (the next day) we put King Ephraim in the ground. Nine men and women went with him, and we all looked very poor.

The slave trade brought enormous suffering and sadness to millions of Africans. Yet the effects of the trade were not the complete disaster for West Africa that some writers have suggested. Close contact between Europeans and Africans stimulated a great increase in trade of all sorts. New goods were brought to the continent and exchanged for raw materials, as well as slaves, and new food crops were introduced from America. And the steady export of people from West Africa may have meant that the population hardly rose beyond a level which food supplies could support. African states were able to adjust to the changing conditions of trade and to exploit new advantages. For example, Dahomey in the mid-eighteenth century had a slave-based economy and wars were waged 'to catch men' who were then sold to Europeans at Whydah. When the slave trade was abolished Dahomey's exports were severely hit, but the country's economy didn't collapse. Instead of being sold, slaves were now put to work on plantations producing palm oil which became a more profitable export than men.

And what happened to Equiano? He was more fortunate than most slaves. By the time he was twenty-one he had been freed by a kindly master. He accepted Christianity, settled in Britain, married a white girl, and wrote a very popular autobiography. Although Equiano travelled widely, to Greenland, Central America, and through the Mediterranean, and was also active in the anti-slavery movement and schemes to settle the 'black poor' in West Africa, he never achieved his ambition to return to his native land. It is doubtful whether he would have enjoyed it for he had become very much an English gentleman.

4 With soft sweet talk

Africa in the early nineteenth century

1804 Start of the Muslim reformist *jihad* in the Western Sudan by the Fulani warrior-scholar Uthman dan Fodio (1754–1817) who conquered Hausaland and founded the Sokoto Caliphate. Islam spread over a large part of the interior of West Africa during the nineteenth century.

1806 Mungo Park died on his second expedition to explore the Niger. The British occupied, and eventually annexed, the Dutch colony at the Cape.

1808 The United States and Britain made it illegal for their citizens to engage in the slave trade. Britain attempted to suppress the slave trade in West Africa and across the Atlantic.

1818 *Mfecane* raged in south-east Africa and Shaka became the ruler of the Zulu.

1820 Mohamed Ali's Egyptian army conquered the Nile Valley.

1822 Afro-Americans who had returned to West Africa established Liberia.

1830s The French captured Algiers and began the long struggle to conquer and settle Algeria. In southern Africa Bantu-speaking groups moved northwards across the river Limpopo and into central Africa where Mzilikazi established the Ndebele state. Boers trekked away from Cape Colony and set up their own republics in Natal, and then the Orange Free State and the Transvaal. In southern Nigeria the Fulani defeated the once powerful Yoruba empire of Oyo. This was followed by a succession of wars in Yorubaland which continued until the 1890s.

West African ivory in a London warehouse.

1840 Seyyid Said moved the capital of his Omani Empire from Arabia to Zanzibar; development of trade routes from the coast of East Africa into the interior and a big increase in the trade in slaves and ivory.

1851 Al-Haj Omar (1794–1864) started his *jilhad*, or holy war, on the upper Niger and with the use of firearms traded from Europeans at the coast he created the powerful Tokolor Empire.

1857 Heinrich Barth and David Livingstone both published accounts of their explorations in Africa.

Abandoned slaves.

1860s Creoles — the black educated elite of Sierra Leone — increased their influence as traders and missionaries along the coast of West Africa; Samuel Crowther became the first black bishop of the Niger in 1864 and later another creole, Samuel Lewis, received a knighthood from Queen Victoria.

1862 John Speke reached the source of the Nile at Lake Victoria.

Sickness plagued white explorers in Africa. Grant continuing his search for the Nile when ill.

1868 Fante chiefs and educated Africans on the Gold Coast created the short-lived Mankessim Confederation.

Curiosity, courage and contempt: explorers in Africa

The nineteenth century was the great age of European exploration of Africa. At the beginning of the century knowledge of the interior was slight. The courses and sources of the great African rivers —the Niger, Nile, Congo and Zambezi, were unknown, while the snow-capped mountains and lakes of East Africa were dismissed by serious-minded Europeans as vague travellers' tales.

With Mungo Park's first expedition to the Niger in 1795 the systematic exploration of Africa began. By 1885 the continent had been crossed from east to west, the extent of the Sahara was known and the major rivers had been followed and mapped. Some explorers were financed by organizations with scientific interests like the African Association, or by governments that were interested in trade and the suppression of the slave trade; but many were lone travellers who combined discovery with trade, hunting and missionary activity. Their motives were mixed; some had an insatiable curiosity, others a desire for fame, wealth or Christian converts.

Throughout the nineteenth century the European and American public were kept well informed about African discovery by the books, lectures and controversies of explorers and the appeals of missionaries. Men such as Livingstone and Speke, whose discoveries caught the enthusiasm of the public, became household names, and yet much of the knowledge about Africa was added by explorers who were not widely known. For example, Benjamin Anderson, a black man who explored the hinterland of his native Liberia in 1868, did not discover any great mountain ranges or impressive waterfalls, but by careful observation and methodical map-making opened up a large area of West Africa. Livingstone and Stanley are justly famous for their crossings of the continent, but the first journey across Africa was made in the early years of the nineteenth century by two Afro-Portuguese traders, or *pombieros*, who kept a rough journal of their lengthy and dangerous expedition.

The greatest danger for explorers was disease. In the nineteenth century West Africa became known as the 'white man's grave' because of the high death rate, particularly from malaria. During the Niger expedition led by Richard Lander in 1832–3 forty out of forty-nine members died from disease; on a much larger expedition in 1841 two-thirds of the Europeans died, half of them within the first two months. Although quinine was known and spasmodically used it was only after Dr William Baikie's successful use of the drug on his Niger expedition of 1854 without any loss of life that its value was generally recognized as a means of preventing and curing malaria. Occasionally explorers encountered hostile Africans. In the Muslim parts of Africa Christian travellers could be in constant danger and it was wise first to acquire an intimate understanding of Arab life and to assume disguise. Even then some of these bold and daring men were imprisoned or murdered. During his first expedition Mungo Park was robbed, reduced to near nakedness and held captive under dreadful conditions by a Muslim chief named Ali: 'Never did any period of my life', Park later recorded, 'pass away so heavily; from sunrise to sunset I was obliged to suffer with an unruffled countenance, the insults of the rudest savages on earth.'

At the same time it must be remembered that many European explorers travelled great distances through Africa with only a few black companions and frequently found only curiosity, food and shelter from the people through whose country they went. Africans must have been puzzled by lone white men wandering around and Mungo Park tells of a friendly merchant asking 'with great seriousness what could possibly induce me, who was no trader, to think of exploring so miserable a country as Africa'. All explorers in one way

Stanley's search for Livingstone. Some European exploring expeditions were large well-organized affairs with hundreds of black porters to carry food, trade goods and supplies.

or another relied upon Africans as guides, interpreters, guards and porters. The selection of porters to carry stores and trade goods demanded tact and careful judgement on the part of the explorer; without their loyalty and cooperation an expedition could be reduced to ruin and perhaps the explorer's life put in great danger. Although some European explorers, like Henry Stanley, were harsh and brutal in their treatment of Africans close contact between individual white and black men frequently created mutual respect and genuine friendship. This same regard was not always extended to African institutions. Richard Lander wrote disparagingly about the Muslim states of northern Nigeria and more or less poked fun at what he regarded as the Africans' inferior way of life. His companion Hugh Clapperton was less arrogant and his account of the peoples of the Western Sudan is both informative and sympathetic.

As European interest in Africa increased in the later part of the nineteenth century many African rulers became more hostile to explorers. They feared that foreign influence and rivalry might weaken their control over trade, or as in the case of the Afro-Arab slave traders in central and eastern Africa, bring it to

an end. In the wake of the explorers came European traders and missionaries and then, by the end of the century, conquest and foreign rule. By 1900 parts of Africa were still unknown to Europeans, shown on maps by the word 'unexplored' across a white area, and exploration of the continent continued into the twentieth century. By this time a number of Africans had also started to 'discover' Europe for themselves. In 1896 Salim bin Abakari, who came from what is now Tanzania, visited Russia and Siberia. Here is part of his account, originally written in Swahili:

When we reached Petersburg I was at once aware that now we were in another country. The clothes there are different from those worn in European countries, and the carriages were of a different kind. Inside, their droskies were very small, and the drivers were dressed like old women. Truly when a person is on a journey he learns many things, and increases his knowledge. The people of Russia have a sterner temperament than other white people. . . . In my opinion the Russians are well behind other white people, because in other white countries every white person is taught to read and write, but in Russia most people do not know how to read, because they do not like studying, and it seems to me it is their laziness.

Explorers

James Bruce
1730–94

The source of the River Nile was one of the great unsolved mysteries of Africa in the eighteenth and nineteenth centuries. What was the origin of this vast expanse of water that flowed across barren desert into Egypt? One of the first Europeans to try to find the answer was James Bruce, a tall, strong, red-haired Scotsman who spoke fluent Arabic, was a crack-shot and a splendid horseman.

Bruce travelled into Ethiopia in 1770 and after many adventures reached a swamp that he believed to be the Nile's source:

'Throwing my shoes off, I ran down the hill towards the island of green turf, which was in the form of an altar, and I stood in rapture over the principal fountain which rises in the middle of it.'

With water from the spring in a coconut shell he toasted his success at having 'arrived at the source of the Nile'.

Unfortunately Bruce had only found the source of the smaller Blue Nile. The main river, the White Nile, flowed from Lake Victoria much farther south.

Francisco José de Lacerda

In 1798 Francisco de Lacerda, a Brazilian mathematician and veteran explorer, died of fever on the shores of Lake Mweru in central Africa. The powerful Lunda king, Mwata Kazembe, refused to allow the Portuguese expedition to go any further and the attempt to cross the continent had to be called off. However, Lacerda's maps and diaries provided later explorers with detailed knowledge of a large area of the interior of Africa.

Mungo Park
1771-1805

'I had', wrote Mungo Park, 'a passionate desire to examine a country so little known and to become acquainted with the modes of life and character of the natives.' In 1795, on a salary of fifteen shillings a day, Park was sent by the African Association to find out which way the River Niger flowed. At that time Europeans failed to realize that the river's delta was the maze of confusing waterways and mangrove swamps along the coast of Benin. Some people, including Park, thought the river flowed west to join up with the Senegal river. Others believed that it went east and either flowed into the Nile or the Congo, or perhaps into a great lake.

Mungo Park's first sight of the Niger is perhaps one of the great moments of African exploration:
'Looking forwards I saw with infinite pleasure the great object of my mission — the long-sought-for majestic Niger, glittering in the morning sun, as broad as the Thames at Westminster, and flowing *to the eastwards*. I hastened to the brink, and, having drank of the water, lifted up my fervent thanks in prayer to the Great Ruler of all things, for having thus far crowned my endeavours with success.'

A scene from Mungo Park's book of his travels.

In 1805 Park led a second expedition down the Niger. All the members either died of disease or were killed in an ambush at the Bussa rapids.

For several more years no more attempts were made to reach the Niger. In 1820 Hugh Clapperton and two companions set out from North Africa to cross the Sahara to the Niger Valley. Clapperton reached Kano and Sokoto, the large and powerful Muslim trading cities in northern Nigeria. The emir Muhammed Bello of Sokoto, a distinguished scholar and statesman, was friendly and helpful but wouldn't let Clapperton go on to the Niger, a mere 150 miles away. However, Clapperton had learnt that the river flowed into the sea. In the next year he returned with Richard Lander, this time coming through the Niger Delta and approaching Sokoto from the south. The course of the Niger was known at last.

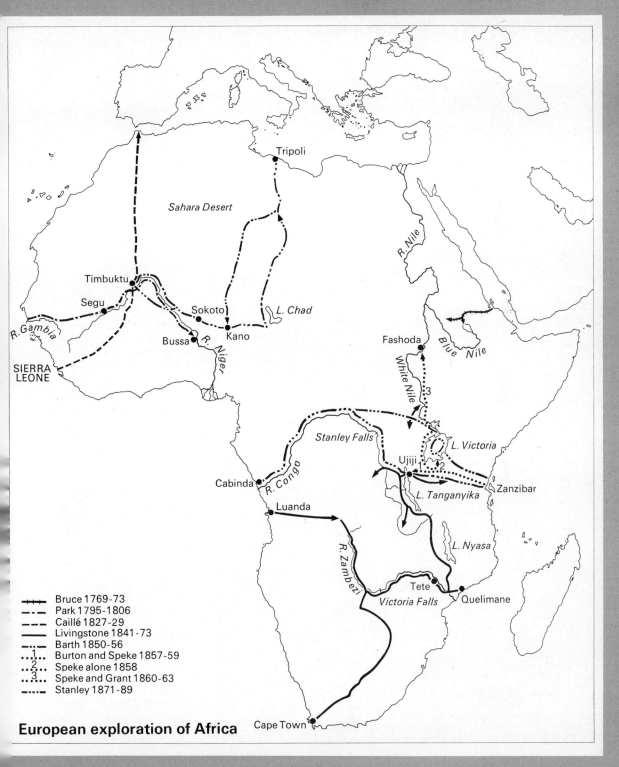

Tripoli

Sahara Desert

Timbuktu
Segu
Sokoto
L. Chad
Bussa *R. Niger*
Kano

R. Gambia

SIERRA
LEONE

R. Nile

Fashoda

White Nile

Blue Nile

3

Stanley Falls

L. Victoria

Cabinda *R. Congo*

Ujiji

Luanda

L. Tanganyika
Zanzibar

R. Zambezi

L. Nyasa

Tete
Victoria Falls
Quelimane

Cape Town

┼┼┼ Bruce 1769-73
─·─ Park 1795-1806
─ ─ Caillé 1827-29
─── Livingstone 1841-73
─··─ Barth 1850-56
···1·· Burton and Speke 1857-59
···2·· Speke alone 1858
···3·· Speke and Grant 1860-63
─···─ Stanley 1871-89

European exploration of Africa

René Caillié
1799—1838

For centuries Europeans regarded Timbuktu as a place of remote mystery. A young Frenchman, René Caillié, was determined to reach the city. In 1828, disguised as an Arab, he entered the city only to find it far different from what he had expected: 'At length, we arrived safely at Timbuktu, just as the sun was touching the horizon. I now saw this capital of the Sudan, to reach which had so long been the object of my wishes. On entering this mysterious city . . . I experienced an indescribable satisfaction. . . . I looked around and found that the sight before me did not answer my expectations. I had formed a totally different idea of the grandeur and wealth of Timbuktu. The city presented, at first view, nothing but a mass of ill-looking houses, built of earth. . . . I found the city neither so large nor so populous as I had expected. Its commerce is not so considerable as fame has reported . . . the market was a desert.'

David Livingstone
1813—73

To the Victorians David Livingstone was a national hero. He was a missionary doctor but also an explorer who mapped a large part of southern Africa. He inspired other explorers, drew public attention to the brutal slave trade in central and eastern Africa, and by his speeches and the manner of his lonely death in the heart of the continent stimulated a new Christian missionary interest in Africa. Livingstone saw Africa as being in

desperate need of the 'civilizing' influence of Europe. 'The usual state of African society', he wrote, 'gives rise to frequent and desolate wars, and the people long in vain for a power able to make all dwell in peace.' Here is part of Livingstone's account of the vicious methods used by Afro-Arab slavers:

'15 July 1871. About 1500 people were in the market at Manyeuma. It was a hot, sultry day. Before I had got thirty yards out of the market, the discharge of two guns in the middle of the crowd told me that the slaughter had begun: crowds dashed off from the place, and threw down their wares in confusion and ran. At the same time that the slavers opened fire on the mass of the people near the upper end of the market place, volleys were discharged from a party down near the creek on the panic-stricken women, who dashed at the canoes. These, some fifty or more, were jammed in the creek and the men forgot their paddles in the terror that seized all. The canoes were not to be got out, for the creek was too small for so many; men and women, wounded by the balls, poured into them, and leaped and scrambled into the water, shrieking. A long line of heads in the river showed that a great number struck out for an island

Timbuktu as drawn by René Caillié.

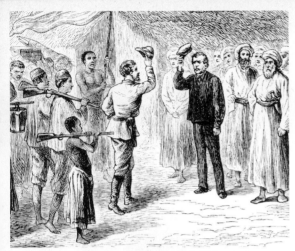

'Dr Livingstone, I presume.' Stanley finds Livingstone.

The last mile of Livingstone's travels.

a full mile off, and many of these inevitably perished. . . . Shot after shot continued to be fired on the helpless and perishing. Some of the long lines of heads disappeared quietly; whilst other poor creatures threw their arms high, as if appealing to the great Father above, and sank.'

Livingstone's remedy for this frightful business was to encourage legitimate trade in the place of the slave trade. European commerce would clear a way for Christianity, and this in turn, he believed, would bring to Africa the vast benefits of modern civilization and progress.

An African village
from Barth's *Travels in Central Africa*.

Heinrich Barth
1821–64

In 1857 the two greatest living explorers of Africa each published a book. David Livingstone's *Missionary Travels* sold thousands of copies and he became a household name; Heinrich Barth's *Travels and Discoveries* had only small sales and he was little known then or today.

Barth was a German, a studious man who had learnt Arabic while still at school. Along with two other Germans he was sent by the British Government, in 1849, to negotiate commercial treaties with rulers in the Western Sudan. He travelled dressed

as an Arab and astride either a camel or a mule. In his baggage he carried a full dress suit which he obligingly put on to show Africans how Europeans dressed. During five years of travel Barth provided a meticulously accurate description of the region between Lake Chad and Timbuktu, an area then hardly known to Europeans. His notebooks are full of detailed information about rivers, towns, trade routes, customs of the people, vocabularies of languages, and descriptions of plants and trees.

Richard Burton
1821—90
and **John Speke**
1827—64

Richard Burton

Burton was a hot-tempered, restless adventurer. He spoke over thirty languages and had become famous by travelling in disguise to the forbidden Muslim holy city of Mecca. Speke was a competent surveyor and keen on big-game shooting. Both men were

Grant dancing with Ukulima, king of the Nyamwezi. Grant and Speke were only two of the many explorers who sought the Nile's source. One explorer, Sir Samuel Baker, was asked by an Nyoro chief: 'Suppose you get to the Great Lake, what will you do with it? What will be the good of it?'

Speke presenting a white rhinoceros to Rumawika, king of Karagwe, 'an ever-smiling man of noble appearance and size'.

eager for the glory of discovering the source of the River Nile.

Together in 1856 they marched inland from the East African coast. Their discoveries and theories sparked off a bitter geographical debate. Burton claimed that the Nile flowed out of Lake Tanganyika, while Speke, who alone had pushed north to Lake Victoria, said he had discovered the true source of the river. In 1860 Speke, accompanied by James Grant, returned to East Africa to settle the matter. This time he went to the north of Lake Victoria, visited the court of Mtesa, the *kabaka* or king of Buganda, and stood beside the fierce waters of the Blue Nile as they poured northward out of the lake.

Speke was correct, but back in Britain the argument over the precise source of the Nile continued for another thirteen years. A public debate between Burton and Speke was arranged in 1864. Speke never reached the meeting. As Burton waited on the platform a message was brought that Speke had shot himself, apparently accidentally, while out shooting game near his home.

Henry Morton Stanley
1841—1904

Stanley's exploits caught the public imagination, but he was never accepted into the Victorian establishment.

There are only two ways of exploring Africa, wrote a missionary: there is the Livingstone way, slow and conciliatory, and the Stanley way, using force and ruthlessness. On all his expeditions —to 'find' Livingstone, the remarkable 999-day crossing of Africa from east to west in 1874—7, on the Upper Nile, and as a servant of King Leopold in the Congo — Stanley used unnecessary force and violence. An African king, Mojimba, described the coming of Stanley down the Congo:

'When we heard that the man with the white flesh was journeying down the Lualaba we were open-mouthed with astonishment. . . . That man, we said to ourselves, has a white skin. He must have got it from the river-kingdom. He will be one of our brothers who was drowned in the river. . . . Now he is coming back to us, he is coming home. . . .

We will prepare a feast, I ordered, we will go to meet our brother and escort him into our village with rejoicing! We donned our ceremonial garb. We assembled the great canoes. . . . We swept forward, my

canoe leading, the others following, with songs of joy and with dancing, to meet the first white man our eyes had beheld, and to do him honour.

But as we drew near his canoes there were loud reports, bang! bang! and fire-staves spat bits of iron at us. We were paralysed with fright; our mouths hung wide open and we could not shut them. Things such as we had never seen, never heard of, never dreamed of —they were the work of evil spirits! Several of my men plunged into the water. . . . What for? Did they fly to safety? No —for others fell down silent —they were dead, and blood flowed from little holes in their bodies. ''War! that is war!'' I yelled. ''Go back!'' The canoes sped back to our village with all the strength our spirits could impart to our arms.

That was no brother! That was the worst enemy our country had ever seen.'

Mary Kingsley
1862—1900

In spite of her black-dressed, prim appearance Mary Kingsley preferred the company of west-coast traders and African villagers to 'the people in London drawing rooms'. In her travels through West Africa, mainly for scientific purposes which she financed by trading with Africans, nothing

seemed to daunt her. She travelled among cannibals, waded chest-deep in swamps, ate snakes, and never fired a single shot in all her journeys. Mary Kingsley described hardship and danger with a sense of humour. On one occasion she fell fifteen feet into a bagshaped animal pit and landed on sharpened sticks:

'It is at these times you realize the blessing of a good thick skirt. Had I paid heed to the advice of many people in England . . . and adopted masculine garments, I should have been spiked to the bone and done for. Whereas, save for a good many bruises, here I was with the fullness of my skirt tucked under me, sitting on nine ebony spikes some twelve inches long, in comparative comfort, howling lustily to be hauled out.'

Mary Kingsley died in South Africa, of a fever, caught while nursing prisoners-of-war during the Boer war.

Vast sums of money and precious lives: missionaries in Africa

The nineteenth century was the golden age of Christian missions in Africa. Why did men and women go as missionaries? A hundred years ago more people were active in the church than today and missions were founded to 'spread the Gospel' at home and overseas. There was a strong belief in the 'saving influences of Christianity' and the Bible exhorted 'Go ye and teach all nations'. The foreign mission field was spoken of as 'duty', 'noble work' and the 'glorious fight', while an Anglican bishop said that 'death for the faith is the greatest blessing a man can meet'. An aura of glamour attached to the work of 'converting the heathen' and even as seasoned a missionary as Livingstone talked of feeling 'exhilarated' by his calling to Africa.

Most missionaries carefully planned their undertakings but a few showed suicidal foolishness in plunging unprepared into the continent. There were many hardships and few comforts and frequently all too few converts to show for years of work. Disease decimated the early missionaries. The wife and two children of Johann Krapf, the German missionary, died within six months of his arrival in East Africa in 1844, and of the 197 members of the Universities Mission to Central Africa between 1860 and 1890 twenty-seven died and forty-five were withdrawn or invalided home. Only a minute handful of white missionaries were killed by Africans and in nearly all cases their deaths can be attributed to either misunderstanding or their own rash and ill-considered actions. Denominational rivalries were transferred from Europe to Africa and led to fierce hostility between missions, each fearing that the other would steal its members and converts. Not all whites thought missions a good thing for Africa. Some traders, administrators and travellers viewed the missionary as a disruptive element whose 'mistaken benevolence' might undermine the ordered traditions of African life and threaten the stability of government and trade.

Many White missionaries in the nineteenth century shared the cultural arrogance of the time. They made sweeping and crude generalizations about Africans and institutions such as polygamy and slavery which they condemned as being opposed to 'civilized Christian standards', by which they really meant European standards. This is illustrated by the following story: 'Now that your people have accepted Christianity,' said the missionary to the chief, 'your women ought to cover up their breasts.' The chief was horrified. 'Do you want them to look like prostitutes?' he said.' Although some optimists thought they saw in the Negro race 'a capacity for receiving the truth of the Gospel beyond most other heathen nations', to most missionaries Africans were 'fallen men' living in 'a moral wilderness' a life that was a 'horrible pit of miry clay'. African religious beliefs were dismissed as a mixture of fear and superstition maintained by fraud and ignorance. Islam, that other great rival missionary force of the nineteenth century, was condemned as sensual and base and associated with slave trading, although some missionaries recognized the benefits that it had brought to Africa. Edward Blyden, the distinguished African scholar, regarded Islam as a religion more suited to Africa because it lacked the racial prejudice and cultural intolerance of European Christian missions. During the nineteenth century missionaries frequently supported Africans against various forms of oppression, slavers, ruthless traders and harsh white men, but by the early twentieth century they were less prepared to speak out against the actions of colonial regimes. One missionary in Nigeria reported that Africans were being trained 'to be Christians, and as such loyal subjects of our King'; another in Kenya defended forced labour for Africans, saying this was far better than 'young male natives . . . loafing about the native reserves dressing themselves in paint and feathers and dancing their immoral dances

White missionaries and black converts, Northern Nigeria. Islam, with its own missionary movement, presented a great barrier to the spread of Christianity in Africa. Many colonial administrators also actively discouraged what they regarded as the disruptive influence of Christian missions in Muslim areas such as Northern Nigeria and Southern Tanzania.

to the detriment of themselves and the young women, and therefore of the tribe'.

Because the death-rate among white missionaries in West Africa was so high black missionaries were recommended as being more suited to the climate. Liberated slaves from Sierra Leone were among the first black missionaries, including Samuel Ajayi Crowther, who was eventually to become the first African bishop of the Anglican church. African converts were in many cases the main means of spreading a knowledge of Christianity rather than white missionaries. For example, Christian ideas swept across Buganda during the religious revival of the 1890s when Africans went all over the country 'carrying Gospels and reading sheets'. Inevitably conflict arose between Africans and white missionaries over the question of church leadership. Henry Venn, the wise secretary of the Church Missionary Society, had given some good advice in the 1860s which unfortunately few missionaries followed:

Study the national character of the people among whom you labour, and show the utmost respect for national peculiarities. . .

. . . let a national church be organized as a national institution. . . . Train up the native church to self-dependence and to self-government from the very first stage . . . the proper position of a missionary is one external to the native church.

Stern-faced and determined women missionaries about to set out on a journey. They had to be tough to withstand diseases, insects, and long years of frequently unrewarding work.

Disputes led to splits in the missions and some African Christians either took over the buildings or broke away to set up their own separatist churches. These separatist, or independent churches, represented an early form of religious nationalism which has been called 'Ethiopianism', taken from the text in Psalm 68, 'Ethiopia shall stretch forth her hands to God'. Black American missionaries were active in Africa in the nineteenth century and many of them provided a stimulus to the idea of Ethiopianism, which also had its supporters among the Negro churches in the United States. One of the most prominent was Bishop Turner's African Methodist Episcopal church.

The African reaction to missionaries depended to a large extent upon the political situation. Some tribes feared whites as 'spirits of evil' or as 'supernatural beings and powerful wizards', while the king of the Ijebu people in Nigeria thought white men inferior and swore that he would never shake hands with them. Africans who accepted and cooperated with mission-aries frequently did so, not because they wanted to become Christians, but because they hoped to gain goods and the support of whites against their enemies. Missionaries were used by African kings as secretaries and advisers in negotiations with Europeans. For example, Thomas Birch Freeman acted as an intermediary for the king of Dahomey, while the French missionary François Coillard gained acceptance in Barotseland because its ruler Lewanika saw the advantages to be gained from Western education. There were many African rulers, like Jaja of Opobo, who did not want to have anything to do with missionaries. They feared that the uninvited foreigners would threaten their authority and prestige by interfering with internal politics, trade and social customs. They further disliked the patronizing attitude of white men and understandably were suspicious that European armies would quickly follow after missionaries.

It was not unusual for missions to encourage European intervention in Africa. The British invasion

Part of Revelation 2x in three African languages: Luganda, Teso and Dinka.

Beranga mwesigwa okutusa
okufa, nange ndikuwa engule
ey'obulamu *Kub. 2. 10.*

Kiboyinene lomunot akitodol
atwanare, eoŋ da kainakini
lwaru aboko naka akijara
Apuk. 2. 10.

Ɣe naŋ adot agut thou,
ku yin ba yen gol de pir.
Ny. 2. 10.

of Asante in 1896 was hailed as a 'righteous war', while four years earlier a white clergyman in Lagos had stated:

War is often a means of opening a door for the gospel to enter a country. A sword of steel often goes before a sword of the spirit.

The Kingdom of Buganda in East Africa became the centre of a religious civil war with French Roman Catholic converts pitched against Protestant followers of the Church Missionary Society. The two sides were locally known as Wa-Fransa and Wa-Ingleza — the people of the French and English. Islam and then the rival Christian denominations had entered the country in the 1870s and by the time the eighteen-year-old Mwanga succeeded to the throne as *kabaka*, or king, in 1884, the three religious groups were well established. They were mainly composed of young men whom Mwanga tried to play off against the older chiefs of the country. Mwanga vacillated in his policies in an attempt to strengthen his authority, persecuting then favouring the religious groups which grew steadily more powerful until they assumed a large measure of independence. When in 1888 Mwanga tried to crush them they deposed him as *kabaka*. The Muslims, Catholics and Protestants couldn't agree how the country should be ruled and a three-sided civil war broke out which lasted for four years. The French Catholic missionaries demanded the support of their government and the English Protestants clamoured for Buganda to be taken over by the British. The Wa-Ingleza, who were the smallest faction, gained a dominant position when Lugard in 1892 intervened on their side and used his military force to defeat the Catholic army.

Christian missions have made important contributions to Africa. The study of languages was pioneered by missionaries like S. W. Koelle, who produced his *Polyglotta Africana* in 1854. Medical knowledge, schools, newspapers and industrial skills were, and still are, organized by missionaries who have rarely confined themselves merely to preaching.

Medicines and microscopes: a missionary dispensary in the 1890s. Christian missionaries frequently pioneered programmes of public health. In 1900 Dr Albert Cook, of the Church Missionary Society in Uganda, diagnosed sleeping sickness.

Missionaries

Dr John Philip
1775–1851

Dr Philip arrived in South Africa from Scotland as superintendent of the London Missionary Society in 1820. He protested against the inhuman treatment given to the Hottentots, who were reduced to near slavery, and was largely responsible for gaining in 1828 the Fiftieth Ordinance which recognized the equality of all races before the law.

Bishop Samuel Ajayi Crowther
1806–91

As a boy Samuel Crowther was rescued from a slave ship and landed at Freetown. He was educated in Sierra Leone and England and in 1841 he went on the disastrous expedition to explore the Niger. Crowther was ordained as a clergyman in the Church of England and, along with many other liberated Africans, he went to southern Nigeria to join the Niger Mission at Abeokuta, in his native Yorubaland. He worked hard to extend the work of the mission which he believed would be helped by the expansion of British control in Africa. In 1864 Crowther became the first black bishop of the Anglican church. From then, until his death, he was in constant conflict with Europeans who criticized the way he ran his mission diocese. After 1870 there was a growing dislike by whites of educated Africans and Bishop Crowther's authority was undermined, his suggestions ignored, and eventually he was displaced.

Johann Krapf
1810–56

Krapf was a Lutheran, who worked first as a missionary in Abyssinia and then founded the Church Missionary Society station at Mombasa in 1844. He was joined by two fellow-Germans, Rebmann and Erhardt. Although they had few converts they had 'vision, tenacity and boundless courage', believing that other missions would follow them to East Africa. Krapf and Rebmann explored inland from the coast to the snow-peaked Kilimanjaro and the eastern parts of the Kenya Highlands.

Cardinal Lavigerie
1825–92

Lavigerie was a Frenchman of 'independent character and indomitable will' who became the Roman Catholic archbishop of Algiers in 1867. He founded the White Fathers, a missionary order that worked among Muslims in North Africa. Lavigerie failed in his attempts to establish a mission in the Western Sudan and he then turned his attention to East and Central Africa. In 1878 the White Fathers entered Buganda, an area in which British Protestant missionaries were already active, and within a few years rival groups of African Christians were at war with each other. Lavigerie led a crusade against slavery. He condemned Islam as being partly responsible and called for a private army to destroy the slavers in their strongholds and for European intervention to suppress the trade.

Mary Slessor
1848–1914

A Scottish orphan and mill-hand Mary Slessor went to work for the Presbyterian mission among the Okoyong people of Calabar in southern Nigeria. She lived with the people, ate their food and identified herself with them in an attempt to gain converts, and to end human sacrifices and the killing of twins. Mary Kingsley described her as a woman with 'tact and courage . . . and an influence and power among the Negroes unmatched by that of any other white'. Mary Slessor was popular among Africans and was frequently called 'Ma', and the 'white queen of Okoyong'.

Bishop Samuel Crowther.

Dan Crawford
1870–1926

A member of the Plymouth Brethren and not supported by any missionary organization, Dan Crawford followed the missionary F. S. Arnot to the court of Msiri, the despotic and temperamental ruler of the slave-trading state of Garenganze, in Katanga. Crawford was young — only twenty years old when he arrived in Central Africa — impetuous, and indifferent about his health or his life. He believed that direct dependence upon God and a life of poverty were essential for missionary work, and for over twenty years he lived, worked and tried to think like an African. When Msiri was killed and his empire began to break apart, many Africans turned to Crawford and treated him as a chief. Crawford moved his followers to a new self-governing and self-supporting mission village on the shores of Lake Mweru and earned the name of 'Kongo Vantu' — 'Gatherer of the People'.

Joseph Booth
c. 1850–1928

Booth was a visionary and champion of African rights who went to Nyasaland in 1892 as an independent Baptist missionary. He later became a Seventh Day Adventist and then a member of the Watchtower Movement, or the Jehovah's Witnesses. Booth was a pacifist who believed in equality of treatment for people irrespective of their race. When he advocated 'Africa for the Africans' and petitioned the colonial authorities over African rights he came into conflict with the government and other missions. He befriended John Chilembwe although he was in no way involved in Chilembwe's abortive rising against the British in 1915. Booth was deported from several African territories and generally condemned by white governments and missions as a 'dangerous' influence.

Prophet William Wade Harris
c. 1850–1928

A Methodist-educated preacher from Liberia, Harris arrived in the French colony of the Ivory Coast in 1913. Dressed in a flowing white robe, sandals, and a white turban, and carrying a rough wooden cross, Harris claimed: 'I am sent by Christ and nothing shall prevent me from accomplishing the deeds to which he calls me. I am going through this country, driven by inspiration from On High. I must bring back the lost nation to Christ. . . .' Preaching through an interpreter he denounced traditional African religion and in one year converted over 100,000 people to his particular brand of Christianity. At first the French authorities tolerated Harris because he preached one God and loyalty to the government, but when his followers began to demand political rights they deported the prophet back to Liberia.

William Wade Harris.

Murder of Bishop Hannington by the soldiers of King Mwanga of Buganda in 1886. Despite this popular image of constant danger very few missionaries or travellers were killed by hostile Africans.

Back to Africa

For over two hundred years black men in America have thought of returning to Africa. In 1780 the blacks in the United States numbered half a million, about one-fifth of the population, while there were possibly over 20,000 in Britain, mainly former slaves. Africa had an emotional pull for black men as the land of their origin, but it also offered a possible place of escape from the racial discrimination of white society. Lott Carey (1780—1828), a black American missionary who sailed to West Africa in 1820, said:

I am an African, but in America, however meritorious my conduct and respectable my character, I cannot receive the credit due to either. I wish to go to a country where I shall be estimated by my merits, not by my complexion.

Whites saw free Negroes as a problem. In America they were regarded as 'a dangerous and useless element', and in Britain, because of their poverty, as a burden on the system of poor relief. Granville Sharp and Olaudah Equiano, the former slave, supported a scheme to resettle the British 'black poor' on the coast of West Africa and in 1787 the colony of Sierra Leone was founded. They also hoped the colony would be of benefit to British trade. Thirty years later a small party of black American immigrants supported by the American Colonization Society and the US Government settled on the coast of what is now Liberia. Many Negroes opposed emigration and the great abolitionist Frederick Douglass (1817—95) stated emphatically that the black man should not leave America, that country they had helped to build. 'We live here,' he said, 'have a right to live here, and mean to live here.'

During the nineteenth century other schemes were put forward by blacks for settlements in Africa. Martin Delany (1818—85), a journalist and doctor, led a party to the Niger Valley in 1859—60 in order to negotiate for land and make treaties. Nothing came of this plan, or his earlier grand proposals for a black colony on the coast of East Africa which would grow rich by trading with Asia and be linked by a railway to West Africa. Delany was the first important American Negro nationalist, and he thanked God that he was black. Another Afro-American who took pride in his race and colour and looked to Africa was Alexander Crummell, a thin, eloquent clergyman who was an early exponent of what we know today as negritude. In his sermons and tracts Crummell argued that the Negro was destined to emerge as a superior race with 'a great work to do in Africa':

The kings and tradesmen of Africa, having the demonstration of Negro capacity before them, would hail the presence of the black kinsman from America, and would be stimulated to a generous emulation. To the farthest interior, leagues and combinations would be formed with the men of commerce, and their civilization, enlightenment and Christianity would be carried to every state, and town, and village of interior Africa.

Between the Civil War and the early years of the twentieth century the most outspoken supporter of black emigration was Bishop Henry Turner (1834—1915) of the African Methodist Episcopal Church. Turner's political ambitions had been constantly baulked by white prejudice and in his bitterness he announced that black men must emigrate to the 'promised land' of Africa and there set up their own nation:

I see nothing for the Negro to attain unto in this country. . . . He can return to Africa, especially to Liberia where a Negro government is already in existence, and learn the elements of civilization in fact . . . there is nothing in the United States for the Negro to learn or try to attain to.

Largely due to Turner's support for this dream and his idealizing of Africa, as well as the alienation and despair of Negroes in America, 'Africa fever' reached its peak in the 1890s, although only a few black men actually emigrated to Liberia.

Marcus Garvey.

The Indispensable Weekly
The Voice of the Awakened Negro—The Peerless Paper

Guaranteed Circulation 50,000
Reaching the Mass of Negroes Throughout the World

The Negro World

ONE GOD, ONE AIM, ONE DESTINY

A Newspaper Devoted Solely to the Interests of the Negro Race

VOL. VIII. No. 24   NEW YORK, SATURDAY, JULY 31, 1920   PRICE: THREE CENTS IN GREATER NEW YORK, FIVE CENTS ELSEWHERE IN THE U. S. A. TEN CENTS IN FOREIGN COUNTRIES

GREAT WORLD CONVENTION OF NEGROES

Members of the Race From All Parts of the World to Assemble at Liberty Hall, New York, Sunday, August 1, at 10 A. M.—Biggest and Most Representative Assemblage in History of the Race

CONSTITUTION OF NEGRO LIBERTY IS TO BE WRITTEN

The intellectual voice of black America in the twentieth century was William Du Bois (1868–1963), a confident cosmopolitan scholar who had been a founder member of the National Association for the Advancement of Coloured People in the US and who in his old age emigrated to Africa to become a citizen of the newly independent Ghana. Du Bois (pronounced Boys) was an active organizer of the early Pan-African Congresses held in Europe before and after the First World War. He felt Africa to be his 'fatherland' and in his autobiography he explained that

the real essence of this kinship is its social heritage of slavery; the discrimination and insult; and this heritage binds together not simply the children of Africa, but extends through yellow Asia and into the South Seas. It is this unity that draws me to Africa.

There was no love lost between Du Bois and Marcus Garvey (1887–1940), the vain, turbulent, jet-black tub-thumper from Jamaica who preached 'Africa for the Africans, at home and abroad' in the black slums of North America. Garvey saw himself as a 'race leader' and through his very successful Universal Negro Improvement Association he gave many blacks a pride in their colour as well as uniforms, parades and pageantry. The ultimate solution for the black man, said Garvey, was to return 'home' to Africa, and as proof of his belief in this he formed the Black Star Steamship Line to transport the emigrants. In 1920, at the height of his power, he declared himself to be the provisional President of the African Republic and told a mass meeting in New York:

The Negroes of the world say, 'We are striking homewards towards Africa to make the big black republic.' And in the making of Africa a big black republic, what is the barrier? The barrier is the white man; and we say to the white man who now dominates Africa that it is to his interest to clear out of Africa now, because . . . we are coming 400,000,000 strong, and we mean to retake every square inch of the twelve million square miles of African territory belonging to us by right Divine. . . . We are out to get what has belonged to us politically, economically, and in every way.

Garvey's organization collapsed in 1925 when he was imprisoned for fraud. He died in London poor and forgotten but his movement had stirred black men to a new consciousness which contributed to their demand for black civil rights in America over the last twenty years.

The poet Aimé Césaire, from the French-speaking West Indian island of Martinique, has since the late 1930s been the main exponent of negritude. Negritude is a philosophical idea which says that black men, whether they be in Africa or America, have a special way of thinking and feeling which non-Negroes do not have. Because the black man has been despised and harshly treated, Césaire argues, he is in danger of resenting his blackness but what he must do is take a pride in his colour; therefore black is beautiful. The idea of negritude has most support among French-speaking black intellectuals.

5 A plague of Europeans

Rulers and ruled. Europeans recruited black troops to conquer and maintain authority in their African colonies. British officials and soldiers of the West African Frontier Force in Nigeria in the 1890s.

Africa in the late nineteenth century

1869 Suez Canal opened.

1874 Asante invaded by the British.

1879 Zulu war: the power of the once-powerful Zulu armies broken by the British. In West Africa Samori Touré, the ruler of the Manding Empire, began his long struggle against the invading French.

Zulu soldiers, 1879. They had guns but relied on spears in battle.

1881—2 Arabi Pasha's nationalist government in Egypt was overthrown by the British who occupied the country. The French seized Tunisia.

1884—5 Congress of Berlin: increase in the 'scramble' for Africa by European powers. Leopold of Belgium founded the Congo Free State. Expansion of Christian mission activity in Africa.

1886 Gold discovered in the Transvaal.

1887 King Jaja of Opobo deposed by Harry Johnston who further extended British control over southern Nigeria.

1890 Religious war in Buganda between Catholic and Protestant factions.

1893 Lobengula's Ndebele state conquered by the forces of Cecil Rhodes's British South Africa Company. French completed their conquest of the Tokolor Empire in West Africa.

1896 Ethiopians defeated an invading army of Italians at Adowa.

1896—7 Revolt by Shona and Ndebele against white settler rule in Southern Rhodesia. In West Africa the British conquered Asante and Benin and the French Dahomey and the Ivory Coast. Fante chiefs and educated Africans in the Gold Coast formed the Aborigines' Rights Protection Society to act as watch-dog of African interests.

1898 Egyptian—British army conquered the Mahdist state in the Nile Valley. At the battle of Omdurman 11,000 Sudanese were killed while the invaders' dead numbered forty-eight.

1899 Outbreak of Boer War in South Africa, which continued for three years.

Boer soldiers.

1900 Sokoto Caliphate in northern Nigeria invaded and overthrown by British army led by Frederick Lugard. Revolt in Asante against British misrule. Rapid expansion of cocoa production by African farmers in the Gold Coast.

1905—7 Maji Maji war against Germans in Tanzania.

1906 Zulu revolt in South Africa against white-imposed taxes.

1908 Belgium takes over the Congo Free State after an international outcry against white methods of rubber collection.

1910 Union of South Africa formed by whites.

1912 African National Congress formed in South Africa. France occupied Morocco and Italy took Libya from Turkey.

1914 Blaise Diagne elected as the first African to represent Senegal in the French Chamber of Deputies in Paris. First World War broke out.

Western conquest of Africa in the late nineteenth century

During the early years of the nineteenth century Western Europe had a growing interest and involvement in Africa. The dominating question was the suppression of the slave trade which Britain and the United States had made illegal for their subjects by 1808. Britain tried to extend the ban to other countries in Europe and also to get African rulers to stop supplying slaves. Most African rulers were more interested in making a living than in humanitarian ideals and they were suspicious at the sudden change of policy and resentful of attempts by Britain to stop the trade. 'Hitherto,' said a West African King, 'we thought it was God's wish that Black people should be slaves to White people. White people first told us we should sell slaves to them, and we sold them; and White people are now telling us not to sell slaves. If White people give up buying, Black people will give up selling.' Although the transatlantic slave trade did not come to an end until the mid-1860s, 'legitimate' trade goods such as palm oil gradually replaced the exports of human beings from West Africa.

'If we really wish to do good in Africa, we must teach her savage sons that white men are their superiors.' James MacQueen, a British geographer, 1821

Words such as 'savage', 'lazy', 'superstitious', 'brutal', 'cruel', 'barbaric', 'stupid' and 'bloodthirsty' punctuate the white man's literature about Africa in the nineteenth century. With few exceptions European travellers, missionaries and anthropologists regarded Africans as an inferior race of people living a degraded way of life in a dark continent. Sir Charles Dilke expressed a typical view in the 1860s:

Africa is distinguished from every country under Heaven by its misery and degradation . . . and lying, as of old, in the outer darkness.

Nineteenth-century Europeans, surrounded as they were by their technological achievements, had the confident belief that these benefits should in the name of 'civilization' and 'progress' be imposed on Africans, by force if necessary. 'It may be,' wrote the great anti-slavery improver Thomas Buxton in 1839,

that . . . a thousand nations now steeped in wretchedness, in brutal ignorance and devouring superstition, shall under

Mungo Park, the Scottish explorer, regarded the Africans of the interior of West Africa as superior to the 'degraded' people of the coast. But, as this passage from his Travels *shows, he thought Africans and Europeans to be in many ways equal to one another:*

When we arrived at the blacksmith's place of residence, we dismounted and fired our muskets. The meeting between him and his relations was very tender; for these rude children of nature, free from restraint, display their emotions in the strongest and most expressive manner. Amidst these transports, the blacksmith's aged mother was led forth, leaning upon a staff. Everyone made way for her; and she stretched out her hand to bid her son welcome. Being totally blind, she stroked his hands, arms and face with great care, and seemed highly delighted that her latter days were blessed by his return, and that her ears once more heard the music of his voice. From this interview I was fully convinced that, whatever difference there is between the Negro and European in the conformation of the nose and the colour of the skin, there is none in the genuine sympathies and characteristic feelings of our common nature.

This picture from a missionary magazine shows Africans as simple people.

British tuition emerge from their debasement, enjoy a long line of blessings — education, agriculture, commerce, peace, industry and the wealth that springs from it.

Most whites assumed a natural superiority over blacks. Their paternal conduct towards those they regarded as 'inferior', 'primitive' and 'childlike' varied considerably. Livingstone stressed the responsibility of 'consistent moral conduct . . . sympathy, consideration and kindness' in dealings with Africans, while at the other extreme the explorer Stanley seemed to take a pleasure in imposing his will by force on black men. Many Europeans felt they had to prove their dominance and leadership by displays of energy and acts of courage. For example, F. C. Selous, the hunter, recorded that when his porters refused to retrieve a couple of dead hippos from a crocodile-infested river he swam out to get them 'if only to show the natives that a white man will do what they dare not attempt'.

Certain Africans were admired by Europeans for their martial qualities. The Zulu were the favourites and Rider Haggard painted a romantic picture of them in his novels; Kipling in his poem 'Fuzzy-Wuzzy' tries to give the views of an ordinary soldier about the Sudanese peasants who fought the British in the Nile valley in the 1890s.

So 'ere's to you, Fuzzy-Wuzzy, at your 'ome in the
    Soudan;
You're a pore benighted 'eathen but a first-class fighting
    man;
An 'ere's to you, Fuzzy-Wuzzy, with your 'ayrick 'ead of
    'air —
You big black boundin' beggar — for you broke a British
    square.

The African response

Africans on the west coast adapted to the new economic and political conditions that came from closer contact with whites. Some black kings and merchants embraced European culture, spoke and wrote French or English — one even had a subscription to *The Times* — built western-style houses and adopted the uncomfortable and inappropriate dress of Europe. For a good part of the nineteenth century most Africans succeeded in maintaining their independence by diplomacy, and by playing one group of Europeans off against another. Many were astute businessmen who were able to gain the advantage over their European competitors. In the interior of the continent one or two rulers of large states had a false idea of their power. For example, Muhammad Ahmad the Mahdi who raised a *jihad* in the Sudan, hoped to conquer the world and demanded not only the surrender of the Egyptians but also of the British and French. Ahmadou Sekou, who became ruler of the Tokolor Empire in 1862, was more realistic and tried to establish trade relations with Europeans at the coast, although perhaps he would have been wiser to have discouraged them as did other kings, who feared the whites become 'strong enough to seize on the country and disposses its rulers'. Eventually the Tokolor Empire was overrun by the French.

West African intellectuals

On the West African coast a small number of black intellectuals wrote and debated about Africa's future political and social development.

James Africanus Horton (1835–83), a doctor and army officer from Sierra Leone, dreamt of an independent Africa. He denounced the popular racialist nonsense about the inferiority of Africans and argued that given the help of western Christian civilization, with its economic advantages and education, black people were capable of governing themselves. He saw the possibilities in his own country:

It is evident that there is growing at Sierra Leone an enlightened population, and that under the fostering care of the mother Government the people can, within a short time, be left to govern themselves; that with an enlightened monarch, elected by universal suffrage, and an efficient legislation, the African element, so essential to African civilization, will receive a powerful impetus to intelligent progress, and raise their much-abused race and country in the scale of civilized nations.

Edward Wilmot Blyden (1832–1912) was born in the West Indies and emigrated to Liberia. He became a teacher, scholar, clergyman and ambassador to London. Blyden took a fierce pride in being a pure-blooded Negro, for he believed that the races of mankind had been created equal but different and each with a distinctive contribution to make to human civilization. The African races, he stated, had in modern times 'filled a very humble and subordinate part in the work of human civilization. But the march of events is developing the interesting fact that there is a career before this people which no other people can enter upon.' The important contribution of Africa to the world, he suggested, might be 'some of the greatest marvels which are to mark the closing periods of time'.

It may yet come to pass that when, in Europe 'God has gone out of date' . . . then earnest inquirers after truth leaving the seats of science and the 'highest civilization', will take themselves to Africa to learn lessons of faith and piety.

The 'child-like' African

In the nineteenth century many Europeans looked upon Africans as simple, child-like people. This idea was put forward in novels and other books. G. A. Henty was a prolific writer of boys' adventure stories and one of his characters said of Africans:

'. . . They are just like children . . . always laughing or quarrelling. They are good-natured and passionate, indolent, but will work hard for a time; clever up to a certain point, densely stupid beyond. The intelligence of an average Negro is about equal to that of a European child of ten years old. A few, a very few, go beyond this, but these are exceptions, just as Shakespeare was an exception to the ordinary intellect of an Englishman. They are fluent talkers but their ideas are borrowed. They are absolutely without inventive power. Living among white men their imitative faculties enable them to attain a considerable amount of civilization. Left alone to their own devices they retrograde into a state little above their native savagery.'

Winwood Reade, a freelance writer and traveller who visited West Africa, believed in the evolution of man to a state of perfection. In his broad history of civilization, The Martyrdom of Man, *published in 1872, he argued that Africans had further to develop than more advanced light-skinned races:*

'The hunters return, and their friends run out to greet them as if they had been gone for years, murmuring to them in a kind of baby language, calling them by their names of love, shaking their right hands, caressing their faces, patting them upon their breasts. . . . And so they toy and babble and laugh with one another till the sun turns red, and the air turns dusky, and the giant trees cast deep shadows across the street. . . . A European Government ought perhaps to introduce compulsory labour among the barbarous races that acknowledge its sovereignty. . . . Children are ruled and schooled by force, and it is not an empty metaphor to say that savages are children.'

...ns in a mixture of European and traditional dress about 1900. A Nigerian king has adopted a crown and his chief ...ers 'toppers' (above). Regal Nigerian ladies in Victorian finery with their husband (below left). A Basuto chief and his ...below right).

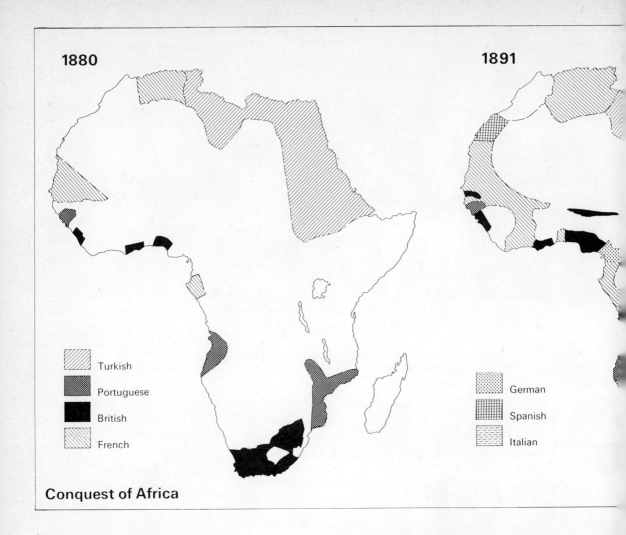

1880

1891

Turkish

Portuguese

British

French

German

Spanish

Italian

Conquest of Africa

'A plague of Europeans'

In the middle years of the nineteenth century missionaries and occasionally merchants urged further European intervention in Africa, but the 'scramble' for the continent was still several decades away. Not all Europeans were convinced about the value of 'civilizing' black men, and governments did not wish to incur the expense or the responsibility of more colonial possessions. In 1865 a British Parliamentary committee resolved that in West Africa

all further extension of territory . . . or new treaties offering protection to any native tribes would be inexpedient; and that the object of our policy should be to . . . transfer to

Africans the administration of all the Governments with a view to our possible withdrawal from all, except, probably, Sierra Leone.

However, by the late 1870s, European commercial and strategic interests in Africa had increased and within twenty years a few powers had divided the continent between themselves. A few people condemned colonial conquest but public opinion, enthused with the idea of empire, took more notice of the arguments used to justify intervention in Africa. European rule, it was argued, would end slavery, tribal warfare and human sacrifice and introduce commerce, Christianity and eventually civilization.

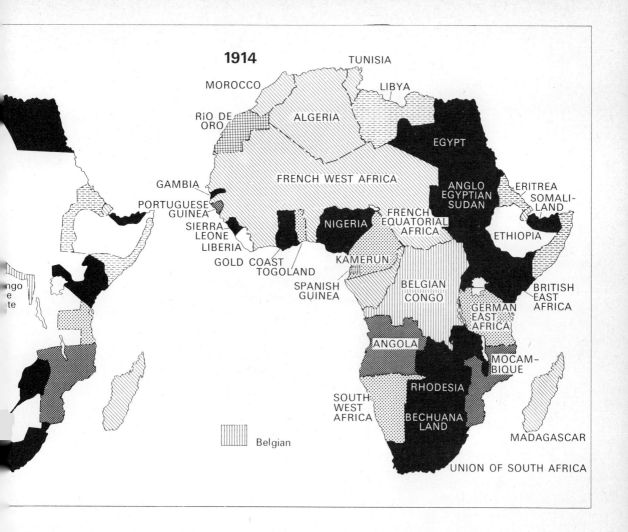

1914

MOROCCO
TUNISIA
LIBYA
RIO DE ORO
ALGERIA
EGYPT
GAMBIA
FRENCH WEST AFRICA
ANGLO EGYPTIAN SUDAN
ERITREA
SOMALI-LAND
PORTUGUESE GUINEA
SIERRA LEONE
NIGERIA
FRENCH EQUATORIAL AFRICA
LIBERIA
ETHIOPIA
GOLD COAST
TOGOLAND
KAMERUN
SPANISH GUINEA
BELGIAN CONGO
BRITISH EAST AFRICA
GERMAN EAST AFRICA
ANGOLA
MOCAM-BIQUE
SOUTH WEST AFRICA
RHODESIA
BECHUANA LAND
MADAGASCAR
UNION OF SOUTH AFRICA

Congo
e

||||| Belgian

Africans reacted in different ways to European intervention. Some rulers attempted to exploit European rivalries. The King of Kiama, in southern Nigeria, wrote to Lugard complaining that the French 'come into this country as if it were a heathen country . . . they are too strong for me and I pray that you will come between me and them'. African chiefs who accepted European treaties of protection did so in an attempt to preserve some measure of independence, gain an ally against neighbouring black enemies, or to keep more ruthless whites from claiming their country. Treaties were frequently meaningless to Africans and disregarded by Europeans when they became incon-

venient. Throughout the whole continent Africans fought against the white invaders. Although they were sometimes successful in battle they lacked unity and in the long run were unable to withstand the superior weapons of Europeans.

When the Germans, supported by a few spurious treaties and warships, took over Tanganyika in the 1880s they arrogantly disregarded the customs and traditions of coastal society. An Afro-Arab trader named Abushiri who, we are told in a Swahili poem, 'was brave as a lion and intolerant of oppression', started a revolt. The poem goes on to say of the Germans: 'They wanted all the towns; indeed they had bought them. At Kilwa and Dar es Salaam there was a plague of Europeans. There was no free speech; they held all the country.' The rising was crushed and Abushiri captured and hanged in 1889.

The European mistreatment and conquest of Africa is perhaps best summed up in this poem that comes from Salaga, Northern Ghana, written in Arabic in 1900. Here are a few lines from it:

I've set out this poem in rhyme. . .
For the profit of intelligent folk. . .
Anyone with brains will heed it.
From our words,
He'll grasp our intention.
A sun of disaster has risen in the West,
Glaring down on people and populated places.
Poetically speaking, I mean the catastrophe of the
   Christians,
The Christian calamity has come upon us
Like a dust-cloud.
At the start of the affair, they came
Peacefully,
With soft sweet talk.
We've come to trade!! they said,
'To reform the beliefs of the people',
'To halt oppression here below, and theft',
'To clean up and overthrow corruption,'
Not all of us grasped their motives,
So now we've become their inferiors.
They deluded us with little gifts
And fed us tasty foods . . .
But recently they've changed their tune . . . .

Pink cheeks

Colonial rule imposed foreign laws and customs on traditional African society. Chief Kabongo of the Kikuyu, one of the peoples of Kenya, describes the coming of a white administrator to his people in the early years of this century:

A Pink Cheek man came one day to our Council. . . . He came from far, from where many of their people lived in houses made of stone and where they had their own Council. He sat in our midst and he told us of the King of the Pink Cheek who was a great king and lived in a land over the seas. 'This great king is now your king,' he said, 'and this land is all his land, though he has said you may live on it as you are his people and he is your father and you are his sons.' This was strange news. For this land was ours. . . . We had no king, we elected our Councils and they made our laws. . . . With patience, our leading Elders tried to tell this to the Pink Cheek, and he listened. But at the end he said, 'This we know, but in spite of this what I have told you is a fact. You have now a king . . . and in the town called Nairobi is a Council or government that acts for the king. And his laws are your laws. . . .

Under colonial rule Africans had their land taken from them by white settlers, they were made to pay taxes, grow certain crops, and forced to work for the government. The secretary of the Kenya Colonial Association argued in 1908 that the government should not only provide settlers with land but also force Africans to work:

It is grossly unfair to invite the white settler to this country as has been done, to give him land under conditions which force him to work, and at the same time to do away with the foundation upon which the whole of his enterprise and hope is based, namely, cheap labour, whilst the native is allowed to retain large tracts of land on which he can remain in idleness.

Colonial rule

Many colonial territories in Africa were vast and there were few white officials or troops to govern them. An administrator in Kenya in 1902 summed up his situation in his diary:

Here we are, three white men in the heart of Africa, with twenty nigger soldiers and fifty nigger police, sixty-eight

British invasion of Asante, 1874. The well-organized army of Asante was defeated. The king fled and his capital, Kumasi, was burnt down. The war cost the British taxpayer £760,000. At home the taxpayer was kept informed about the colonial wars by engravings like these from the *Illustrated London News*.

Human sacrifice was part of the religious ritual of several West African states. European travellers in the nineteenth century exaggerated the number of sacrifices and confused graveyards with slaughteryards. *Right:* Sir Garnet Wolseley entering Kumasi. *Below:* The king's slaughtering place discovered during the campaign.

African policemen supervised by white officers maintained the host of new laws and regulations introduced by colonial regimes. Water police, Natal, South Africa, 1902.

The highest authority in a colony was the Governor. Below him were a succession of white District Commissioners and Officers. Sir William Maxwell, Governor of the Gold Coast 1895—8, on tour.

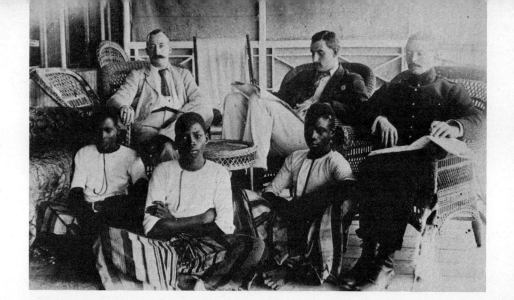

Europeans and servants, 1900.

miles from doctors or reinforcements, administering and policing a district inhabited by half a million well-armed savages who have only quite recently come into contact with the white men . . . the position is most humorous to my mind.

Lugard's solution to this problem in northern Nigeria was to govern through traditional African rulers. This system of indirect rule, or 'native authorities', as they were later to be called, became one common method of government in both some British and French colonies. The traditional rulers had limited power; real control lay with the colonial authorities which, said Lugard,

are to be obeyed in all matters whatsoever. . . . Every Sultan and Emir and the principal officers of the State will be appointed by the High Commissioner throughout all this country. The High Commissioner will be guided by the usual laws of succession and the wishes of the people and chiefs but will set them aside if he desires for good cause to do so. The Emirs and Chiefs who are appointed will rule over the people as of old time . . . but they will obey the laws of the Governor and will act in accordance with the advice of the Resident.

And the white Resident 'adviser', supported by a force of troops, was constantly at hand to see that the African ruler maintained the 'pacification, good government and progress' of his province.

The European powers had different ways of govern-

ing their colonial territories but their main interest was the economic exploitation of the continent. Economic development in African colonies was to this end. Railways, roads and bridges were built so that minerals and cash crops could be brought to the coast for export; schools were opened to train clerks and artisans; attempts were made to control disease and improve methods of agriculture to get better financial returns from investments. At the same time it is important to remember the selfless work of many who worked in the colonial service and who genuinely had the interests of the African at heart. But, more important, to many Africans the period of alien rule was an unwarranted intrusion into Africa. Writing at the time of Tanganyika's independence in 1961, Julius Nyerere had this to say of colonial rule:

Our whole existence has been controlled by people with an alien attitude to life, people with different customs and beliefs. They have determined the forms of government, the type of economic activity — if any — and the schooling which our children have and . . . even if they have always done their best to do what they believed to be good for us (and I do not believe it is possible for any set of people all the time to submerge their own interests under those of the people they control), it would be no less wrong. A man who tries to control the life of another does not destroy the other any the less because he does it, as he thinks, for the other's benefit. It is the principle which is wrong, the principle of one man governing another without his consent. . . .

'To strike a blow and die'

Africans continued to resist Europeans in a variety of ways right throughout the colonial period. Armed resistance led to bloody repression and the leaders of rebellions were frequently labelled as 'fanatics' or given titles such as the 'Mad Mullah of Somaliland'.

'The Germans treat us badly and oppress us much,' an African schoolgirl in Southern Tanzania wrote in 1898. Eight years later many of the people of Southern Tanzania united to fight the Germans in what has come to be known as the Maji Maji War. The cause of the war was the brutal administrative methods of the Germans, but it was sustained by African leaders and became a mass movement through the use of popular religious beliefs. Africans believed that if they drank a mixture of maize and sorghum seed mixed with *maji* (water) they would be immune from the bullets of the Europeans.

The Germans crushed the rising using African auxilary troops from tribes not involved in the rebellion. As many as 100,000 people may have died in the fighting and the famine that followed the war. However, to a small number of Africans European control was welcomed for the advantages it brought. Three years after the Maji Maji War an African teacher wrote:

The Lord God give the Kaiser strength and power to accomplish all that happens in the land. . . . Formerly its condition was one of injustice. . . . But now there is peace everywhere.

An imperial incident, 1887

'My first and last words are that the country belongs to me and I do not want white traders there. Anyone who wishes to trade with me must do so at my port of Opobo.' So wrote Jaja, king of Opobo, to Lord Granville, the British foreign secretary, in 1882.

Jaja, a former slave, had established a powerful state at the mouth of the river Niger which controlled the strategic waterways used for the export of palm oil. With a fleet of well-armed war canoes Jaja opposed African and European rivals who threatened his monopoly. He also tried to keep interfering British missionaries out of his state and maintain his independence. However, when the British declared the Niger delta a British protectorate in 1885 his days as an independent ruler were numbered. Sir Harry Johnston, the British consul, called Jaja 'a cruel and false chief who laughs at Her Majesty's Government' but to break his power would need 'no other display of force than the action of a gunboat'.

On the morning of 19 September 1887, the gunboat *Goshawk* stood off Opobo with its guns prepared for action and seventy armed sailors standing ready. Johnston summoned Jaja aboard and demanded his surrender. Faced with the alternative of having his town bombarded and being hunted as a common criminal Jaja had little choice.

He was tried by a British court and exiled to the West Indies where he lived on a pension of £800 a year. Other African rulers in southern Nigeria were similarly treated and by 1900 the whole of the area had been subjugated by the British and was open to missionary activity, commercial exploitation and foreign rule.

New subjects for African wood carvers: Kaiser Wilhelm and Queen Victoria.

Submission to the new rulers. King Prempeh kneels before the British governor after the British had invaded Asante again in 1896.

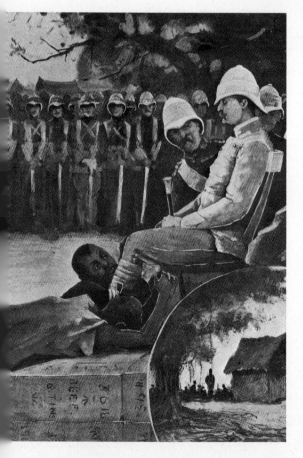

In Nyasaland (now Malawi) in 1915 the Reverend John Chilembwe led a short-lived revolt against British colonial rule. Chilembwe was a remarkable man. He had studied and been ordained as a minister in the United States, and on his return to Africa he formed a separatist church, the Providence Industrial Mission, to be run exclusively by Africans. The Mission had a chain of churches and schools and emphasized the spiritual and economic improvement of the African. Despite his education Chilembwe was still regarded by most Europeans as any other 'native', and missionaries increasingly feared that he was out to 'poach' members away from their missions. Chilembwe actively opposed the land and tax policies of the colonial authorities and in 1914 his final protest was against the recruitment of Africans for the army. 'Let the rich men, bankers, titled men, storekeepers, farmers and land-lords go to war and get shot,' he argued. 'Instead the poor Africans who have nothing to own in this present world . . . are invited to die for a cause which is not theirs.' Within two months he raised his revolt. It was ill-supported and although only three whites died Chilembwe was hunted down and shot and many of his lieutenants were either hanged or imprisoned. The revolt appears more as a dramatic gesture to highlight African grievances, an act of martyrdom on the part of John Chilembwe 'to strike a blow and die'.

Samori Touré: 'The Bonaparte of the Sudan'
c. 1830–1900

Samori was our greatest adversary on the African continent. He was the only one who gave proof of those qualities characteristic of a chief of a people, a strategist and even a politician. He was an outstanding leader of men, possessing audacity, energy, the ability to follow up an advantage and plan in advance, and above all an irrepressible tenacity.

A French general wrote these words about Samori Touré, an African ruler who with great skill fought for fifteen years against the French army invading his empire in West Africa. Another French officer was so impressed by Samori that he gave him the highest tribute, calling him 'the Bonaparte of the Sudan'.

Samori was the son of a Manding-speaking farmer who traced his origin from a long line of Muslim traders, or *dyulas*, who were to be found all over the interior of West Africa. At first Samori worked for his father but when he was eighteen he decided to become a trader. As a *dyula* he travelled over a wide area buying and selling cattle, horses, kola nuts and slaves, and also importing firearms and gunpowder from the Europeans on the coast. The many commercial contacts that Samori made among the *dyula* were later to be useful when he set about establishing an empire.

About 1851 Samori's mother was captured by a raiding party of the king of Bissandugu and made into a slave. With great boldness Samori went to the king and offered his services as a soldier in return for his mother's freedom. The king accepted. Samori was a very successful soldier. He quickly learnt the art of war, became an army commander, and such was his personality that warriors were eager to join his efficient, well-equipped raiding force. Samori's position grew so strong that in the 1860s he broke away from Bissandugu and established his own state. One of his aims was to unite all the Manding-speaking kings and chiefs under his leadership and revive the long dead empire of Mali that had thrived in the fourteenth century.

The empire of Samori was a remarkable achievement. By 1880 his personal rule extended from the borders of Sierra Leone across the grasslands of the Sudan to the northern Ivory Coast and included many of the Manding-speaking peoples. Samori governed the empire from his capital at Sanankoro, collected taxes or 'tribute' from his subjects, and used the army to maintain peace and authority. A French officer who visited the empire in 1887 said that

every village can appreciate its new well-being and relative security; for it now has to suffer the tyranny of one man only, and that is softened by the remoteness of Samori, who is constantly trying to direct the material and moral affairs of his subjects for the best.

In an attempt to strengthen his control Samori declared himself to be the *almami*, the religious head of a Muslim state, and commanded that mosques be built in every town and village. He also encouraged children to learn the Koran and ensured that

his rule is carried out by unexpectedly summoning, and personally interrogating some child of good family, even from the most distant part of his empire. If the child's ignorance shows that he has not been following the Muslim teacher a heavy fine is imposed on the parents.

The key to Samori's power was the well-organized army dispersed throughout the provinces of the empire. The regular army was composed of disciplined young infantrymen who carried rifles and who were known as the *sofa*. Many of the soldiers were captives of previous wars. In addition there was a military reserve in all the villages and towns which could be called upon in emergency. These soldiers were highly efficient and although there was only a small group of cavalry they could easily and quickly be moved from one part of the country to another to put down revolts or protect the frontiers. With his knowledge of trade routes and his *dyula* friends, whose commercial interests he protected

Samori was able to have a constant supply of horses, food and firearms for his troops.

Samori faced frequent rebellions and wars but the greatest threat to his young empire was the French on the Senegal river. Up to the last quarter of the nineteenth century European countries had only a few coastal possessions in Africa. However in the 1880s, as trade and military rivalry between the European powers increased, a 'scramble for Africa' developed, with Britain, France and Germany trying to seize as much of the continent for themselves as they could. The French, who already controlled parts of Senegal and Algeria and a few other small trading stations, now began to push an army inland towards the Niger valley and into Samori's empire. Along with other Africans the Manding fought against the foreign invaders but Samori soon realized that his *sofa* were no match in open battle against the better-armed French troops. He therefore changed his tactics and began to train small groups of highly mobile raiders who attacked French forts and supply lines. When the French disrupted the supply of guns and spare parts to Samori's army, blacksmiths throughout the empire were organized to make serviceable replacements so that the fight could continue. The war proved to be a stalemate and Samori offered to sign a peace treaty with the French. Several treaties were agreed to and Samori hoped that by diplomacy he could protect his independence. However the French military were only playing for time. They intended to establish a protectorate over the

Samori Touré

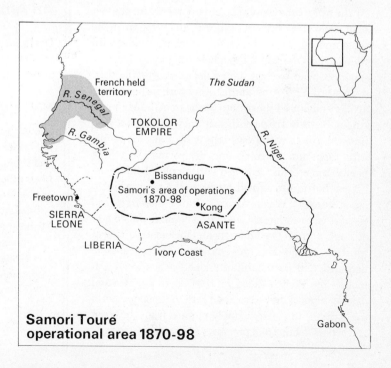

Samori Touré operational area 1870-98

Manding empire and their policy was summed up by Major Archinard, the new commander in the Sudan in 1889, when he said, 'Samori must be got rid of.'

The French encouraged revolts inside the Manding Empire and supported the northern state of Sikasso which was engaged in a bloody war with Samori. Samori was anxious to avoid war with the French and he tried without success to gain British protection for his country and also to make defensive alliances with neighbouring African states. In a letter to Ahmadou Sekou, the ruler of the Tokolor Empire, he wrote:

If you continue to make war on your own, the whites will have no trouble defeating you. . . . Let us therefore unite. You will hit the French from the North, I will harass them in the South, and we will certainly manage to get rid of them.

At the same time Samori began to prepare for the last fight. Gold and ivory were exported to Freetown on the coast and exchanged for modern repeating rifles with which to arm the *sofa*. Throughout the empire the army was organized to fight a long defensive guerilla war.

In April 1891 Archinard's army with its lumbering artillery advanced slowly into the heart of the Manding empire. Within six days the capital was captured and Samori's troops withdrew to the east taking the people with them and burning and destroying everything behind them. This 'scorched earth' policy held up the French but it also earned for Samori a reputation for great cruelty. Weak African states that opposed Samori were ruthlessly treated. The mud-walled city of Kong, with its five minarets and its long tradition of Muslim scholarship, was besieged and completely flattened and its inhabitants killed or enslaved. Although the French failed in 1894—5 to encircle and destroy Samori they were able, with the cooperation of the British, to cut his supply of guns from the coast and separate him from potential African allies such as Asante.

Inevitably, Samori could not hope to win against the superior technical power of the Europeans, but he was unwilling to accept a French protectorate. The *sofa* still won some battles and caused the French large losses but as they retreated they left a desolate waste-land.

In the end Samori made a tactical mistake. He moved his army into the hill forests of Liberia during the rainy season where there was little food to be had. Famine struck and the once loyal *sofa* that had numbered 35,000 men, now exhausted and dispirited faded away. In 1898 Samori was ambushed and captured by the French. He was deported to Gabon on the coast where he died two years later from pneumonia.

An African view of colonialism

David Diop, the author of this poem, was born in France of African parents in 1927. He was killed in an air crash in 1960.

MARTYR

The White Man killed my father,
My father was proud,
The White Man seduced my mother,
My mother was beautiful.
The White Man burnt my brother
   beneath the noonday sun.
My brother was strong.
His hands red with black blood
The White Man turned to me;
And in the Conqueror's voice said,
'Boy! a chair, a napkin, a drink.'

> David Diop, in Olumbe Bassir (ed.),
> *An Anthology of West African Verse.*

Transport in colonial Nigeria in 1910.
For the official à rickshaw, for the
doctor a special railway vehicle.

Frederick Lugard: 'Officer and gentleman'
1858–1945

Frederick Lugard was responsible for establishing British rule over Uganda and conquering northern Nigeria. He believed white men to be superior to black and thought that the extension of European control over Africa would be a good thing. British rule in Africa, he argued, was necessary to end the slave trade, prevent tribal warfare and safeguard missionaries; new lands would be opened to trade and Britain's strategic and economic interests protected by preventing African territories falling into the hands of European rivals.

Early on the morning of the first day of 1900 Lugard hoisted the Union Jack at the town of Lokoja on the Niger while an African military band of the newly formed Frontier Force played 'God Save the Queen' The flag and the proclamation of annexation meant little to the Hausa peasants and their Fulani rulers in the *emirates* of northern Nigeria. To them the Europeans were invaders who should be resisted as non-Muslims — as infidels. The Sultan of Sokoto, the Caliph Attahiru, was recognized by all the other *emirs* as the spiritual and political ruler of the north. His reply to Lugard was brief and defiant:

I do not consent that anyone from you should ever dwell with us. I will never agree with you, I will have nothing ever to do with you; between us and you there are no dealings except as between Muslims and unbelievers — war as God Almighty has enjoined on us. There is no power save God on high.

From their mud-walled towns the armies of the *emirs*, or rulers, came out to fight for their faith and freedom. Peasant foot soldiers dressed in skirts of indigo blue and armed with hardwood bows and iron spears formed

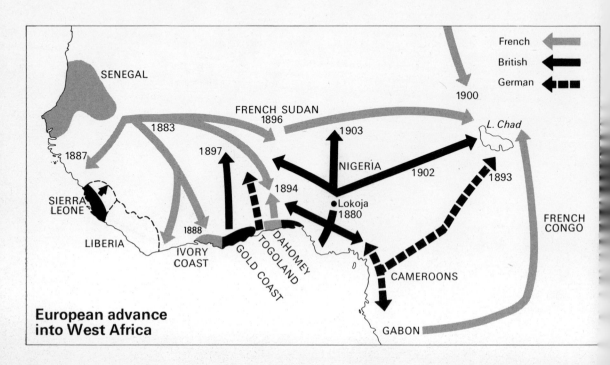

French
British
German

SENEGAL

FRENCH SUDAN
1896

1883

1887

1897

1903

1900

L. Chad

NIGERIA

1902

1893

1894

SIERRA LEONE

Lokoja
1880

FRENCH CONGO

LIBERIA

1888

IVORY COAST

GOLD COAST

TOGOLAND

DAHOMEY

CAMEROONS

GABON

**European advance
into West Africa**

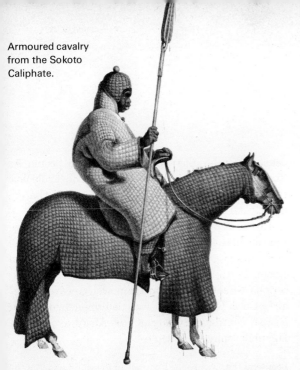

Armoured cavalry from the Sokoto Caliphate.

Lugard

the backbone of the Caliph's forces; a few had fire-arms but little idea of how to use them. The elite shock troops were horsemen, sword and axe-wielding riders, protected by cotton padded armour as were their stallions, and with brightly coloured turbans adorned by feathers on their heads. They flung themselves bravely against the howitzers, machine guns and rifles of the European-led troops, with devastating losses. A report of a battle by a British official says:

They came at us, and the horsemen gave way and went back. No one took any notice. I thought we were all going to be killed. Someone gave an order. Everyone fired, then a whistle blew, everyone stopped and there was no horsemen left alive in front.

The Caliph fled from Sokoto pursued by the British, and rather than surrender he fell fighting like a medie-val knight surrounded by the bodies of over six hundred of his followers. Lugard declared that British rule over northern Nigeria was by right of conquest. In olden times, he told the defeated Fulani rulers, they had conquered the country and taken 'the right to rule over it, to levy taxes, to depose kings and create kings', but now they 'in turn have by defeat lost their rule which has come into the hands of the British'.

Lobengula: King of the Ndebele
d. 1894

A tall, heavily built man, a roll of blue cloth and a bundle of monkey skins around his waist, and a staff in his hand, walked upright through his *kraal* of Bulawáyo. Lobengula, the king of the Ndebele (or Matabele), looked every inch a warrior-ruler. Although his callous cruelty horrified European visitors to his court he could also be an amiable drinking companion and 'appear pleasant and good tempered'. He was shrewd and under no illusion about the designs of Europeans on his country. 'What use is missionary teaching?' he once asked. 'The white men can read and write, but it doesn't make them good.'

The Ndebele kingdom was established in the grasslands north of the river Limpopo, in what is now Rhodesia, by Lobengula's father, Mzilikazi. He had fled with his people, in the 1830s, away from their Zulu overlord and the advancing Boers in South Africa. The Ndebele brought with them the revolutionary military techniques of the Zulu — the disciplined regiments of young warriors carrying short stabbing spears, or *assegais*, who ran into battle in a crescent-shaped formation to envelop the enemy with the two horns — that brought terror to the neighbouring subject Shona people whom they constantly raided for cattle, women and children. When Lobengula became king in 1868 he faced two major problems which threatened the security and unity of his kingdom. Inside the country powerful groups of warriors opposed his succession and supported a rival claimant to the throne, while from outside, increasing numbers of European hunters and traders were pushing north into Central Africa, many of them looking for gold. For twenty years Lobengula used all his political skill and diplomatic cunning in an effort to consolidate and maintain his power over the Ndebele. Fearing that the incoming whites might support his black opponents he bought them off with mining concessions which were too small to endanger his country's sovereignty, or

cause an anti-foreign reaction among his people. As 'the friend and ally of the white men' Lobengula now turned against his black enemies and, in a brief battle, quickly crushed them.

However, by the late 1880s, the 'scramble for Africa' was on and Lobengula's kingdom, astride the vital route into Central Africa, was threatened by rival Boers, Portuguese, Germans and Britons. The most serious threat came from the power-greedy millionaire, Cecil Rhodes, who was determined to extend British control over as much of Africa as possible. His philosophy was simple:

I contend that we are the first race in the world and that the more of the world we inhabit the better it is for the human race. I contend that every acre added to our territory provides for the birth of more of the English race, who otherwise would not be brought into existence. . . I believe it to be my duty to God, my Queen and my Country to paint the whole map of Africa red, red from the Cape to Cairo. That is my creed, my dream and my mission.

Rhodes, a parson's son, was born in England in 1853. Because of poor health he went to South Africa where, within a few years, he amassed a vast fortune from the diamond mines at Kimberley. He was dynamic and aggressive in his pursuit of empire and he now had the cash to pursue his dreams of grandeur. Rhodes had little regard for Africans and envisaged a white confederation of southern Africa and a railway running all the way from Cape Town to Cairo through British-held territory. Essential to this scheme was control over the lands of the Ndebele and Shona in which, it was believed, were large deposits of minerals.

In 1887 the Boers signed a non-aggression treaty with Lobengula. The British feared that the Boers might control central Africa and they hastily made a treaty with Lobengula who, trying to balance one group of whites against another, agreed not to make

Cape Town connected to Cairo by telegraph, 1892. *Punch* cartoon showing Rhodes, who was then Prime Minister of Cape Colony, standing astride the continent he tried to dominate. His other egotistical dream, a railway running from the Cape to Cairo through British territory, was never realized. Today there is still no rail link between North and South Africa.

concessions without the consent of the British. He was now in a very awkward position with his country a 'British sphere of interest'. More and more white prospectors and concession seekers were entering his kingdom and Lobengula realized that his state might be overwhelmed by Europeans in the same way as his African neighbours, to the south. At the same time he had to restrain the militant young warriors, the *matjaha*, who were eager to kill all the whites and who breathed scornful rebellion at the king's conciliatory policies. Lobengula knew that war would mean an invasion by white soldiers and the inevitable destruction of his army which could never stand against machine guns.

In an attempt to solve both of these problems Lobengula, in 1888, signed the Rudd Concession with Rhodes's British South Africa Company, which gave the commercial company exclusive mining rights in the Ndebele country. Lobengula hoped that this would exclude other white men from his lands, while he expected the Company to come, mine for gold, and then go away. There is little doubt that the white agents for the British South Africa Company, in league with Rhodes, deceived Lobengula. The king could not read or write and he signed the concession with a cross, and promises made by the Company during the negotiations were not written into the document. According to the Reverend Charles Helm, a missionary at the king's court, the Company 'promised that they would not bring more than ten white men to work in his country. . . and that they and their people would abide by the laws of the country and in fact be his people. But these promises were never put in the concession.' Helm had no reason to lie about this for, without exception, missionaries regarded Lobengula as 'warlike and cruel' and a 'great obstacle to progress' whose power should be overthrown as quickly as possible. When Lobengula realized that the Company interpreted the concession as a right for large-scale mining, and also white settlement, he tried to renounce the agreement. In a message to Queen Victoria he said: Lodzi [Rhodes] paid me money for which I gave him a piece of ground to dig. If you have heard that I have given my whole country to Lodzi, it is not my word. It is not true. I have not done so. Lodzi wants to take my country by strength.

Left: Africans had to pay taxes to support colonial regimes. Magistrates in South Africa collecting the hut tax. Frequent protests and revolts against taxes occurred throughout Africa.

Right: Cecil Rhodes watching the shelling of enemy positions in the Matabele War, 1896. Drawn by Melton Prior, the special artist sent by *the Illustrated London News* to cover the uprising.

Rhodes, however, had influence and money and he gained from the British Government a royal charter for his Company which empowered it to set up an administration and govern the concession lands. Time was running out for Lobengula. To the missionary, Helm, he summed up his tragic plight:

Did you ever see a chameleon catch a fly? The chameleon gets behind the fly and remains motionless for some time, then he advances very slowly and gently, first putting forward one leg and then another. At last, when well within reach, he darts his tongue and the fly disappears. England is the chameleon and I am that fly.

In July 1890 an armed 'Pioneer Column' of the chartered Company entered the land of the Ndebele, crossed into Mashonaland, and raised the British flag at Fort Salisbury. Lobengula was still anxious for peace and he sent a group of warriors with a message to the Pioneers:

Has the king killed any white men that an *impi* [war party] is collecting on his border? Or have the white men lost anything they are looking for?

The blood of the *matjaha* was up and Lobengula could not keep the respect of his people if he allowed his country to be marched over by white men who ignored his authority. Nor was it possible that European settlers and miners, who employed Shona labourers, would tolerate the traditional Ndebele raids on the Shona for cattle and women. Both black and white wanted a showdown. At last violence broke out. Warriors of an Ndebele raiding party were shot, at Fort Victoria in July 1893, and Lobengula prepared for a war that he could not win. His crack regiments were cut down as corn before a scythe by the European machine guns before they came within throwing or stabbing distance. A European observer of the battle at Shangani river wrote:

I must record the pluck of these regiments which was simply splendid, and I doubt if any European troops could have withstood for such a long time as they did the terrific and well-directed fire brought to bear on them.

Lobengula fled from his *kraal* to the Zambezi valley where he died, a sick fugitive, in early 1894. The power of the *assegai* was broken and the white man now ruled the grasslands as a conqueror.

6 Regaining independence

Independence celebration in Upper Volta, 1960.

Africa since 1914

1914 First World War. Several hundred thousand African troops fought in colonial armies. Allies conquered German territories, including Tanganyika and South-West Africa, by 1918.

1915 John Chilembwe's revolt against British rule in Nyasaland.

1922 Egypt independent but British troops still occupied the country. The former German colonies became League of Nations mandates. South Africa became the mandatory power of S.W. Africa and Britain for Tanganyika, 'responsible for the peace, order and good government of the territory . . . to promote to the utmost the material and moral well-being and the social progress of its inhabitants'.

1923 White settlers in Southern Rhodesia given home rule.

1924 Abd el Krim proclaimed the 'Rif Republic' in Morocco and defeated a Spanish army. He was overthrown by the French and sent into exile.

1930 Portugal's 'Colonial Act' tied the colonies 'to closer communion with continental Portugal'. In 1951 the colonies were declared integral parts of Portugal as 'Overseas Provinces'.

1935 Italian invasion and conquest of Ethiopia.

1939 Second World War starts in Europe. Fighting in North Africa. Many African troops served in Africa and overseas.

1944 Brazzaville Conference: France rejected the idea of autonomy for its colonies and stressed the traditional policy of assimilation, i.e. of making Africans good Frenchmen. The French Union of 1946 gave the colonies local representative bodies and also the right to elect members to the National Assembly in Paris.

1945 Sixth Pan-African Congress held in Manchester. Unlike the previous congresses which had been organized by black Americans and West Indians, this one was dominated by Africans who included Jomo Kenyatta and Kwame Nkrumah. The Congress stated: 'We demand for Black Africa autonomy and independence. . . . We are determined to be free.'

1947 Nationalist revolt against French rule in Madagascar ruthlessly repressed. 20,000 people estimated killed.

1948 National Party in power in South Africa introduces policy of apartheid.

1952 Army officers seize power in Egypt. By 1956 the new regime led by President Nasser had negotiated the withdrawal of British troops from the Suez Canal. Mau-Mau rebellion against white rule broke out in Kenya. A few Europeans and many Africans were killed.

1953 White-dominated Central African Federation set up against African wishes.

1954 Algerian war of independence began. After eight years of violent and brutal fighting France agreed to independence despite the opposition of many European settlers (*colons*) and a section of the French army.

1956 Britain and France attacked Egypt in an attempt to overthrow President Nasser and prevent the nationalization of the Suez Canal.

1957 Ghana became the first British colony in Africa to win her independence.

1958 Guinea voted against membership of the French Community and became independent.

1960 Sharpeville shooting. Congo crisis and division of African states into rival blocs. Most French territories became independent.

1961 Start of Angolan war for independence against the Portuguese. Other wars broke out in Portugal's African colonies of Guiné (1963) and Mozambique (1964). The three wars continue today.

1963 Pan-African Conference in Addis Ababa set-up the Organization of African Unity. The OAU successfully arbitrated in a number of inter-African disputes and consistently opposed white rule in South Africa. Conflicting national policies and personalities have prevented the Organization from achieving the continental unity of which some Africans dream. The Central African Federation was dismantled.

1965 Rhodesia's Unilateral Declaration of Independence from Britain.

1967 Arusha Declaration in Tanzania. Civil war in Nigeria. The Federal Government defeated the breakaway state of Biafra by 1970.

1971 Thousands massacred in Burundi after an unsuccessful revolt against the government.

1972 General Amin expels British Asians from Uganda. Fighting on Uganda—Tanzania border.

Chaos in the Congo

We must lose no chance of securing for ourselves a share in this magnificent African cake.

King Leopold II of Belgium, 1877

In 1885 the United States and a dozen European countries agreed in Berlin to recognize the rule of a private international Association over a large area of the Congo basin. By a stroke of a pen the founder of the Association, King Leopold of Belgium, became absolute ruler of a vast private African estate. The signatories at Berlin believed that European rule would benefit Africans. Opening the conference, Otto von Bismarck, the German Chancellor, declared:

All the Governments invited here share the desire to associate the natives of Africa with civilization, by opening up the interior of the continent to commerce, by furnishing the native with the means of instruction, by encouraging missions and enterprises so that useful knowledge may be disseminated, and paving the way for the suppression of slavery.

George Washington Williams, a black American pastor, newspaper editor, politician and lawyer was commissioned by the US Government in 1890 to investigate conditions in the Congo Free State. Here is part of his report:

'Your Majesty's Government is excessively cruel to its prisoners, condemning them for the slightest offence, to the chain gang. . . . Often these ox-chains cut into the neck of the prisoners and produce sores about which the flies circle, aggravating the running wound. The poor creatures are frequently beaten with a dried piece of hippopotamus skin, called a *chicote*, and usually the blood flows at every stroke when well laid on.'

These fine ideals were soon forgotten. Leopold expected his new and expanding possession to pay its way and he encouraged the exploitation of the resources and the people of the Congo Free State. Taxes were squeezed from Africans and they were forced to collect wild rubber and ivory; if they failed to deliver the required amounts they faced possible flogging, mutilation, and even death. A British consular agent described in 1899 the way in which a State Official used his African soldiers to collect rubber:

His method was to arrive in canoes at a village, the inhabitants of which invariably bolted on their arrival; the soldiers landed and commenced looting; after this they attacked the natives and seized the women; these women were kept as hostages until the chief of the district brought in the required number of kilogrammes of rubber.

Ivory traders, Congo Free State.

The Congo Atrocities caused an international outcry and in 1908, the year before Leopold died, the Belgium Government took over the Congo.

The Belgians administered their newly inherited colony through a Governor-General who was controlled from Brussels. Their main interest was the economic exploitation of the Congo and they continued Leopold's policy of giving commercial concessions to min-

The Congo 1960

ing and railway companies. For example, Katanga in south-east Congo, a mineral-rich province the size of Britain, was dominated by the Union Minière du Haut Katanga, a large trading concern that accumulated assets worth hundreds of millions of pounds. Belgium and company rule was a system of paternalism that excluded Africans from participating in the processes of government. The long-term aim of the Belgians was for Africans to develop at 'their own pace' and that slowly a middle class would emerge that would cooperate in governing the country. The educational system emphasized this. There was a large number of primary schools, run mainly by Roman Catholic missions, and a high level of literacy, but little provision for secondary or higher education. Thus, when independence came suddenly and calamitously in 1960, the Congo had few trained administrators and not one African doctor, lawyer or architect. Racial discrimination was officially illegal and Africans who achieved a certain level of education could be recognized as *évolués*, that is, persons who had evolved towards a civilized stage. But in the growing, overcrowded towns

of Léopoldville and Elizabethville the *évolué* found in his hunt for employment that the whites had all the best jobs and higher wages, and that schools and housing were segregated. The *évolués* in the towns came together into associations and friendly societies who, one historian has written, formed 'a self-conscious elite, on the margin of European culture and society but denied admittance'.

For years the Belgians had prevented political activity in the Congo but in the late 1950s their policy suddenly changed. All around them in French and British territories African nationalist movements were gaining concessions from the colonial governments. In 1958 General de Gaulle visited Brazzaville, just across the river from Léopoldville, and gave Africans in French Congo control over their own government. This intensified activity among the small groups of *évolués* in the Belgian Congo who had already formed political parties. Some of these parties were based on tribal loyalties and advocated either separatist states or a federal structure for the Congo. The ABAKO, led by Joseph Kasavubu, a former government clerk,

91

Kimbanguism

European rule and missionary influence broke down many of the traditional customs of African society. A chief named Matungi in the Belgian Congo said:
'I have tried to understand the white man and his ways but I can see only harm. What happiness have they brought us? They have forced us to a way of life that is not our own.'

During colonial rule a number of African independent churches developed as breakaway bodies from mission Christianity and in reaction to European influence and control. Today in sub-Saharan Africa there are hundreds of independent churches with a wide range of religious belief and practice. Some are large while others have only local loyalties.

In the Belgian Congo in the early 1920s Simon Kimbangu, a devout Bible-reading Baptist, claimed that he had received heavenly messages and had the power of healing. As his messianic movement grew, particularly among the Bakongo, the Belgian authorities became alarmed. Kimbangu was imprisoned and his followers harassed by Government and missions. Between 1921 and 1956 the Church largely operated underground, meeting secretly in small groups. Today it is known as the Church of Jesus Christ on Earth and claims three million followers. Here is part of the Kimbanguist catechism:

1.   Who is Tata (father) Simon Kimbangu?
Tata Simon Kimbangu is the messenger of our Lord Jesus Christ.
2.   How do we know that Tata Simon Kimbangu is the messenger of our Lord Jesus Christ?
Jesus Christ himself has promised us to ask his Father to send us another consoler to continue with His work (John 14 xii–xviii).
3.   What has Tata Simon Kimbangu realized?
Tata Simon Kimbangu has resuscitated the dead; he made the blind see; he made the paralytic walk; he made the dumb talk . . . (Matthew 8 i–x).
19.   Why is it that the name of Tata Simon Kimbangu is put in the first place –is Tata Simon Kimbangu God?
No, Tata Simon Kimbangu is not God, but God in all epochs chooses a man to enlighten his people (Exodus 3 vii–xvii).

Baptism in an African Jordan. A member of an independent church is immersed in the river, before the other believers, as a public sign of his faith.

represented the interests of the Bakongo tribe who
feared that they would be overwhelmed by the influx
of other tribes into the rapidly growing factories of
Leopoldville. In Katanga, Moise Tshombe, a business-
man, helped form CONAKAT, which drew most of its
support from the Lunda tribe. In contrast, a group of
influential *évolués* led by Patrice Lumumba in 1958
formed the Mouvement National Congolais (MNC)
which demanded a strong, unitary, national government. Lumumba was in his early thirties, a fiery orator,
a good political organizer, but a man of unstable personality. Although he had only received primary schooling he had written a book about the future of the Congo
which showed him as a thoughtful and moderate
nationalist who wanted to cooperate with the Belgians.
At a pre-independence conference in Brussels in
January 1960 he had said:

Chipping down the colonial past.
Congolese workmen dismantling
statues of the explorer Stanley (above)
and King Albert of Belgium (below).

As for the Europeans living in the Congo, we would ask them
to stay and help the young Congolese state. . . . We need
their help. . . . It is with their collaboration that we wish to
create the Congolese nation, in which all will find their share
of happiness and satisfaction.

Under pressure from all directions and against a back-
ground of economic recession, tribal conflict, riots and
increasing anti-white feeling, the Belgians hastily
agreed to independence for the Congo by June 1960.
The Congo was ill-prepared to govern itself. The poli-
ticians had no experience of government, there were no
African army officers, and the administrative system
was still largely controlled by Europeans. An uneasy
coalition between ABAKO and the MNC took over
the country with Lumumba as prime minister and
Kasavuba as president. Within a week of independence the Congo (Zaire since 1972) erupted into
violence and disorder which was to last for several
years. The United Nations was involved and the Congo
became a centre of 'cold-war' conflict and rivalry
between African states.

Personalities
in the Congo crisis

Joseph Kasavubu

Kasavubu was born in 1910 in lower Congo of mixed Chinese-African ancestry. He was a dynamic political organizer who became leader of ABAKO, a separatist Bakongo party. As President of Congo in the difficult years of 1960–65 he was a skilful tactician in maintaining himself in power. He died in 1969.

Patrice Lumumba

A moderate nationalist up to early 1960, Lumumba then began to suspect Belgian intentions for the Congo.

Patrice Lumumba was rapidly adopted as a martyr of imperialist aggression in the Afro-Asian and Communist countries. Mourners in Ghana.

He advocated a centralized Congo state. Sudden power as Prime Minister may have corrupted him; he saw himself as the *national* leader of the Congo: 'I am the Congo, the Congo has made me. I am making the Congo.' He was frenetic, unpredictable, impatient and rude in his dealings with the Belgians, the UN and the African states. He was murdered in Katanga in early 1961.

Joseph Mobutu

Born in 1930, Mobutu was an army clerk, then a journalist and member of the MNC. On independence he became Chief of Staff of the Congo Army. He seized power in September 1960 —the first military coup in black Africa. He again took over government in 1965, and now rules Zaire as president in a very personal style.

Moise Tshombe

Tshombe was president of the 'independent' province of Katanga, which was denounced as 'big business controlled'. He was a suave but astute opportunist whom Conor Cruise O'Brien said was 'something of a chameleon'. Because of his involvement in Lumumba's murder he became an object of hatred throughout Africa. He was kidnapped from exile in Spain and died in an Algerian prison in 1969 aged fifty.

Dag Hammarskjöld

Hammarskjöld was a Swedish diplomat. As Secretary-General he gave 'the United Nations a focus of moral authority which could attract an international loyalty, and use it in the cause of peace and justice' (Conor Cruise O'Brien). Anxious to avoid war in the Congo and under pressure from western governments sympathetic to Katanga he was unsure how to interpret the mandate of the Security Council. He was killed in an air crash in Africa in late 1961.

Conor Cruise O'Brien

An Irish historian and diplomat who, largely because of his sympathy for the Afro-Asian point of view, was appointed UN representative in Katanga to 'report and advise, and to apply the resolutions as *interpreted* by the Secretary-General'. Tshombe called him a liar: 'He's not a bad man — only he doesn't know Africa.' He was determined to act as an 'international civil servant' but was also hostile to Tshombe and his white supporters.

Ralph Bunche

A distinguished black American academic, who was awarded the Nobel Prize for Peace in 1950. During July and August 1960 he was the UN Under-Secretary responsible for administering the UN operations in the Congo. He reorganized the administration and negotiated the withdrawal of Belgian troops from the Congo. He died in 1971.

'Sceptres and crowns come tumbling down.' Tshombe as President of Katanga and in an Algerian prison.

Kwame Nkrumah

Nkrumah was the egocentric Prime Minister and then President of Ghana from 1957 until his overthrow by the army in 1966. He was a close personal confidant of Lumumba during the early months of Congo independence. He tried to restrain and moderate Lumumba's impulsive actions. 'You cannot afford, my brother, to be harsh and uncompromising. . . . Be as cool as a cucumber,' he once wrote. He was a strong Pan-Africanist who favoured unitary government and continental unity. He died in April 1972.

Nkrumah and the Queen during a garden party at Christenborg Castle, 1961.

Katanga and the Congo

'The problem of the Congo is Katanga, and the problem of Katanga is finance, and the problem of finance is Union Minière.'

U Thant, UN Acting Secretary-General, 1961.

Katanga was the richest province of the Congo and although it had only 12 per cent of the country's population it contributed 60 per cent of the revenue. It produced:

8 per cent of the world's copper
73 per cent of the world's cobalt
80 per cent of the world's industrial diamonds
60 per cent of the West's uranium as well as gold, manganese and other minerals

Much of this mineral wealth was controlled by Union Minière. Its interests in Katanga were valued at almost £180 million and extended also to railways, flour mills, cement works, cattle ranching and insurance. The net annual profit from these undertakings was $20–30 million. Well over 80 per cent of commercial production in Katanga was in the hands of Belgian, French, British, Rhodesian and South African firms. Many of the 33,000 Europeans in the province held key positions in the economy and most actively supported Tshombe's secession from Congo.

1960

30 June   The Belgian Congo became independent.

'The Congo constitutes, within its present boundaries, an indivisible and democratic state.'
Loi fondamentale du Congo, Article 6, May 1960
'From today we are no longer your Monkeys.'
Patrice Lumumba, the new Prime Minister of the Congo, in his independence address in the presence of King Baudouin of Belgium.

4 July   Force Publique mutinied against its white officers. Start of panic flight of Europeans from the Congo. Administration broke down.

'It all started when General Jannsens, the Belgian commander, refused to promote Congolese to the rank of officer.'
Patrice Lumumba

11 July   Belgian paratroops flown into Congo. Disturbances flared up throughout the country.

'Our action is not aggression . . . it is an action justified by the fact that the Congolese Government was incapable of re-establishing order. Our troops intervened to protect the lives and honour of our fellow citizens.'
Pierre Wigny, Belgian Foreign Minister

Moise Tshombe declared Katanga independent. He began to recruit foreign mercenary soldiers.

'KATANGA INDEPENDENCE DECLARED' The masquerade of Katanga's 'independence' is becoming daily more pathetic. M. Tshombe, the self-styled president, is today more under the domination of Belgian officials than he was . . . before Congo's independence. His regime depends entirely on Belgian arms, men and money. Without this his government would in all probability be quickly pulled down from within and without. The outline of Belgium's emergency policy for Katanga is now discernible. It is to protect the great Belgian financial stake here and hold a political bridgehead in the hope of a Congolese union amenable to Belgium and the West.'
Eric Downton, *Daily Telegraph* correspondent, 27 July 1960

13 July   Congo appeal to the United Nations for military aid to prevent Belgian aggression.

'The Government of the Republic of the Congo request urgent dispatch by the United Nations of military assistance . . . the Belgian action is an act of aggression against our country. We accuse the Belgian Government of having carefully prepared the secession of Katanga with a view to maintaining a hold on our country.'
Joseph Kasavubu and Patrice Lumumba

14–18 July   UN peace-keeping force (troops from Ghana, Sweden, Ireland, etc.) arrived in the Congo under direction of Dr Ralph Bunche.

'The United Nations Security Council
1.   *Calls upon* the Government of Belgium to withdraw their troops from the territory of the Republic of Congo.

Katanga troops with a mortar and an ice cream.

South African mercenary with nuns rescued from a mission.

2. *Decides* to authorize the Secretary-General to take the necessary steps . . . to provide the Government [of the Congo] with such military assistance as may be necessary. . . .'

UN Security Council Resolution, 13 July.

Prime Minister Lumumba wanted the UN force also to help the Central Government end Katanga's secession.

'The United Nations force is a temporary security force in the Congo with the consent of the Government to help restore law and order. It cannot take the initiative in the use of armed force; it can only act in self-defence. The United Nations cannot interfere in the internal conflicts in the Congo . . . it cannot interfere in the political dispute between Katanga and the Central Government.'

Dag Hammarskjölk, UN Secretary-General, on the impartial role of the UN force in the Congo

23 July Belgians completed their withdrawal from Congo but not from Katanga.

'The UN force must be used to subdue the rebel Government in Katanga.' Patrice Lumumba to Dag Hammarskjöld.
'We do not help the Congolese people by actions in which Africans kill Africans, or Congolese kill Congolese, and that will remain my guiding principle for the future.'

Dag Hammarskjold

12 August UN forces entered Katanga to remove Belgian troops.

15 August Relations between Lumumba and Hammarskjöld grew worse over UN policy towards Katanga. Lumumba refused to negotiate with Tshombe as this might have led to a federal solution; he began to prepare to invade Katanga. Without the knowledge of President Kasavubu and the Congo Government Lumumba appealed to the Soviet Union, which sent military equipment and technical aid; he also asked for the active support of the African states to condemn UN policy in Congo.

23 August   Soviet Union condemned Hammar-skjöld UN policy in Congo.

'Lumumba's mistake was to get caught in the trap of the cold war — the white man's folly.'
Aimé Césaire, the Martinique poet

25–30 August   African states meeting in Leopoldville for the Pan-African Conference supported UN policy and advised that the Katanga crisis be settled by negotiation.

'The United Nations has connived with the deposed President Kasavubu who has become an instrument of imperialist policy. The attempts of the ruling circles in the United States and the other western powers to make use of the flag of the UN in order to intervene in Congolese affairs constitute a flagrant violation of the Security Council's decisions.'
Soviet Government statement, 8 September 1960

5 September   President Kasavubu dismissed Lumumba as Prime Minister. Lumumba announced he had dismissed Kasavubu as President.

'The UN command is working in concert with the NATO powers to discredit the legal government of M. Lumumba. The Secretary-General, Mr Hammar-skjöld, is completely lacking in objectivity.'
Soviet statement at UN, 9 September 1960

14 September   Colonel Mobutu and the Congo army took over the government. He cooperated with Kasavubu but opposed Lumumba.

December   Lumumba arrested by the army on warrant from Kasavubu. His supporters, led by Antoine Gizenga, set-up a rival government in Stanleyville, the Lumumbist stronghold.
African unity split over Congo. Most French-speaking states (the Brazzaville Powers) recognized Kasavubu's Government in Leopoldville. The more radical African states such as Ghana, Guinea and Morocco (the Casablanca powers) supported the Stanleyville Government. President Nkrumah of Ghana hoped that mediation by the African states alone would solve the Congo crisis.

'Once we admit our impotence to solve the question of the Congo primarily with our own African resour-ces, we tacitly admit that real self-government on the African continent is impossible.'
President Nkrumah of Ghana, August 1960

1961

January   Lumumba transferred to Katanga where he was murdered, probably with Tshombe's agreement. Lumumba became a hero in the Afro-Asian and Communist countries.

'Patrice Lumumba's murder is one of the filthiest crimes of imperialism.'
Broadcast from Radio Damascus, Syria

21 February

'The Security Council
1. *Urges* that the United Nations take immediately all appropriate measures to prevent the occurrence of civil war in the Congo, including arrangements for cease-fire, the halting of all military operations, and the prevention of clashes, and the use of force, if necessary, in the last resort.
2. *Urges* that measures be taken for the immediate withdrawal and evacuation from the Congo of all Belgian and other foreign military and paramilitary personnel and political advisers not under the UN Command, and mercenaries.'
UN Security Council Resolution

14 June   Conor Cruise O'Brien, an Irish diplomat, appointed UN representative in Katanga. The UN intended to show Tshombe that it was going to implement the UN Resolution of 21 February.

'I thought it should be possible for a combined effort, pivoting on Hammarskjöld and using the lever of the resolutions, to bring back Katanga into the Republic of Congo without violence . . . I [had] the belief that people behind Tshombe had too much at stake to risk disorder.'
Conor Cruise O'Brien, writing in 1962

2 August   New government of 'National Unity' formed by Cyril Adoula and Antoine Gizenga.

28 August   UN 'Operation Rumpunch' organized by O'Brien to round up foreign mercenaries in Katanga. Growing hostility between the UN forces and the Katangese. Katanga had support from Rhodesia, South Africa and right-wing political parties in Europe.

'TO SAVE KATANGA' 'Our reason for fighting, for which we are ready, is our implacable refusal to hang our heads and give in to the interference and pressure of outsiders, who are as ambitious as they are greedy. Our glory is the spiritiual and material inheritance of our Katanga, a sacred heritage from our fathers.'
Editorial from a Belgian newspaper reprinted in Katanga, 30 August 1961

5 September O'Brien feared that Katanga actions would cause a breakdown in law and order.

'I served notice on Tshombe, in writing, that the actions of his government in provoking inter-tribal hatred were liable to cause civil war, and could therefore, if they continued, involve the application of the Resolution of 21 February, which ... authorizes the "use of force, if necessary, in the last resort". In my opinion, the "last resort" was almost at hand.'
Conor Cruise O'Brien

13 September UN troops attempted to seize control of Katanga. UN forces attacked by Katangese gendarmerie in Elizabethville. The British and French Governments denounced the use of force by the UN. Sporadic fighting continued until December.

'The British Government have always accepted that Katanga should form part of the Congo, but that this should be achieved as a result of official negotiation and not by force.'
British Foreign Office spokesman

18 September Hammarskjöld killed in air crash while flying to Northern Rhodesia to hold peace talks with Tshombe. U Thant of Burma became Acting Secretary-General of the United Nations.

24 November

'The Security Council
8. *Declares* that all secessionist activities against the Republic of the Congo are contrary to the Loi Fondamentale and security decisions and specifically *demands* that such activities which are taking place in Katanga shall cease forthwith.

9. *Declares* full and firm support for the Central Government of the Congo, and the determination to assist that Government ... to maintain law and order and national integrity.'
UN Security Council Resolution

1 December O'Brien resigned from the UN after being told he would not remain as the representative in Katanga.

'My instructions from the late Secretary-General were to effect a breakthrough and end the situation in which a Security Council resolution was being openly flouted [by Katanga]. When I got down to this task I found myself increasingly exposed ... to mounting criticism ... not only from Belgium but from two permanent members of the Security Council, Britain and France.'
O'Brien's resignation statement, 2 December 1961
'The British Government ... allowed its territory [Northern Rhodesia] to be used by Tshombe, as a secure base for his actions against the UN. ... I saw [the British Government] as principally responsible for the survival of the state of Katanga.'
Conor Cruise O'Brien

December UN troops ended secession of Katanga. Lengthy negotiations continued throughout 1962. Moise Tshombe went into exile in January 1963.
The UN forces left the Congo in 1964. Unrest and disorder continued in the country until 1967.

UN troops with captured Katanga guerillas.

The making of South Africa

The first inhabitants in South Africa were Bushmen and Hottentots. By the tenth century A.D. Bantu-speaking peoples had crossed the River Limpopo and gradually they spread throughout a large part of what is modern South Africa.

In 1652 the Dutch settled at Cape Town. Gradually small groups of Dutch migrant farmers, or *trekboers*, extended the frontiers of the Cape and clashed with Africans. When the British occupied South Africa at the end of the Napoleonic Wars increasing numbers of boers trekked northwards in search of independence and land. With their ox-wagons, horses and rifles they conquered the lands across the rivers Orange and Vaal and created small isolated rural republics. The boers gained a reputation for harsh paternalism towards Africans: 'We make them work for us in consideration of allowing them to live in *our* land', said a boer leader in the 1850s.

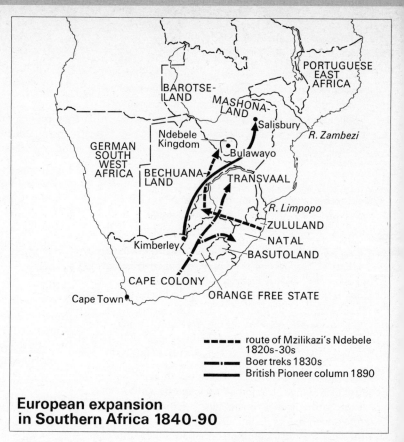

- - - - - route of Mzilikazi's Ndebele 1820s-30s
— · — · — Boer treks 1830s
———— British Pioneer column 1890

European expansion in Southern Africa 1840-90

In the 1820s south-east Africa was ravaged by war, a time known as the *Mfecane* — the Crushing. Out of this violence emerged the powerful Zulu military state led by Shaka. Many Africans fled from the Zulu; Moshweshwe took his people into the safety of the mountains of Basutoland, while Mzilikazi's Ndebele warriors moved northwards into Rhodesia.

The British occupied Natal in the 1840s and soon began to grow sugar. Indentured labourers were brought from India to work on the plantations, and by about 1900, when this picture was taken, they outnumbered the whites in the colony. Today in South Africa there are over 600,000 Asians; they are discriminated against by the white government.

INCIDENTS IN THE TRANSVAAL WAR

BRITISH HOISTING THE UNION JACK AT PRETORIA.

SOUTH AFRICA

ANOTHER LITTLE PATCH of RED.

IF THEY WANT TO GET THE PULL
ON OLD JOHN BULL,
THEY'LL HAVE TO GET UP EARLY
OUT OF BED;
AS AGAIN THEY'VE HAD A SLAP,
WE SHALL PAINT A CERTAIN MAP
WITH JUST ANOTHER LITTLE PATCH OF RED!

In the nineteenth century the 'race problem' in South Africa usually referred to the conflict between Boer and Briton. Tension increased when many British immigrants were attracted into the boer republics of Transvaal and Orange Free State by the discovery of gold and diamonds. Africans were not directly involved in the two wars that the whites fought with each other in 1881 and 1899—1902. This handkerchief shows incidents of the second Boer War. In 1910 the Union of South Africa was created, but this represented the interests of white unity and Africans were ignored.

Industrialization in South Africa began in the late nineteenth century, with simple operations using a few Africans to take the hard work out of panning for gold or digging for diamonds. Today thousands of Africans are drawn to the mines and factories of towns such as Johannesburg and white-owned wealth has become dependent upon black labour. Traditional custom and discriminatory laws segregated people socially and politically by colour. Several small African political groups already existed, but in 1912 these were brought together by Dr Pixley Seme and the Reverend John Duba into the South African Native National Congress (later the African National Congress) to defend African 'rights and privileges'.

The keystone of apartheid is the system of 'self-governing' African territories, or Bantustans. These are eight small fragmented areas comprising just over 13 per cent of the poorest and most rural parts of South Africa designated as tribal 'Homelands' for all Africans who make up over 75 per cent of the population. By 1972 four 'Homelands' had been set up.

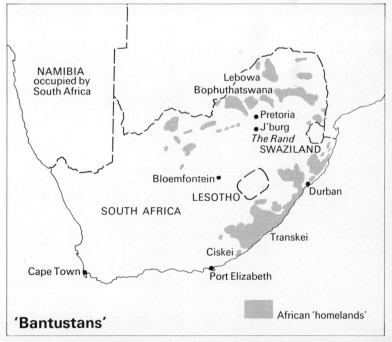

'Bantustans'

African 'homelands'

South Africa: 'A vicious despotism'

In South Africa the non-white is a second-class citizen. Since 1948 the white minority government has through the policy of *apartheid*, or separate development, attempted to rigorously and finally segregate people according to their colour. Today Africans are not allowed to live or work where they choose, they cannot move freely about their country, have no right to marry whom they wish, cannot vote, join a political party or belong to a trade union. Their working conditions and educational opportunities are well below those of white people and they are constantly exposed to arrest by the police for petty breaches of harsh laws. And if Africans protest in any way they can be severely punished. It is hardly suprising that the black nationalist leader, Nelson Mandela, has called this system 'a vicious despotism'.

Nelson Mandela, the eldest son of a chief, was born in the Transkei in 1918. As a young man he came to Johannesburg and there, in the African townships sprawled around the city, he saw for the first time what life was like for Africans who had come from the countryside in search of work in the mines and factories: poverty, police raids for passes, the bulky reference books all Africans have to carry, and job discrimination. Mandela studied hard to be a lawyer and eventually he set up in practice with his friend Oliver Tambo. Both men felt indignant about the way their fellow black men were treated and so they joined the African National Congress, a political movement which fought for African rights. When it was founded in 1912 the ANC hoped to end racial discrimination by agitating for the removal of the colour bar, by petitioning parliament and educating white opinion. The government harrassed black political groups and trade unions and few Africans were prepared for really militant action. An Afrikaans newspaper in 1935 summarized the ineffective politics of the blacks with the headline: 'Naturelle Bly Stil' — 'Natives Stay Quiet'.

A number of younger Africans, including Mandela and Tambo, wanted more positive action and in the early 1940s they formed the ANC Youth League. The struggle against white domination now took a new form. Africans went on strike in the rich mining area of the Rand, illegally squatted on land, boycotted buses, and protested against carrying passes. A new member of Congress, Albert Luthuli, a gentle middle-aged Zulu chief and Christian schoolteacher, summed up the new policy:

At last we began to turn away from thinking in terms of a slight change here and a concession there, and to get down to fundamentals. We began to demand our rightful place in the South African sun.

1948 was a dark year for non-Europeans in South Africa. The Afrikaner-led National Party won the general election and began to impose its policy of *apartheid*. Since the 1920s whites had feared that industrialization and the increasing number of Africans in the towns would lead to the breakdown of the colour bar. The National Party was not only determined to uphold the traditional white policy of *baasskap* (mastership), but to go further and separate the races permanently. Dr Verwoerd, the new Minister of Native Affairs, spelled out what *apartheid* would mean:

The policy will aim at concentrating, in so far as it is possible, the main ethnical groups and sub-groups of Bantu [i.e. Africans] in their own separate territories, where each group will be able to develop into a self-sufficent unit.

In practice this meant a host of laws to control the lives and movements of Africans. By the end of 1950 the government had introduced laws to suppress any opponents it wished by simply labelling them communists, made inter-racial marriages illegal and classified people according to race. Most important

Nelson Mandela after his acquittal in the long treason trial, 1960.

of all, the Group Areas Act was passed giving the government power to move and resettle people in segregated areas. Oliver Tambo, who is now living in exile, has described how the *apartheid* laws caused hatred and frustration and turned numerous innocent people into 'criminals':

Jails are jam-packed with people imprisoned for petty infringements of laws that no really civilized society would punish with imprisonment. To be unemployed is a crime because no African can for long evade arrest if his passbook does not carry the stamp of authorized and approved employment. To be landless can be a crime. . . . To cheek a white man can be a crime. . . . To live in the 'wrong area' — an area declared white or indian or coloured — can be a crime for Africans.

The ANC, now more militant, challenged *apartheid* with a programme of action involving strikes, boycotts and other measures of passive resistance. Africans and Indians came together in 1952 to plan a defiance campaign which, Luthuli explained, involved volunteers publicly disobeying unjust laws 'suffering arrest, assault and penalty if need be without violence'. The volunteers were organized by Nelson Mandela who with his 'natural air of authority was the born mass leader'. On the cold morning of 26 June 1952 the campaign began when thirty Congress members, wearing armbands and shouting *Mayibuye Afrika* —

'Let it come back Africa' — entered the EUROPEANS ONLY entrance of the railway station near Port Elizabeth. They were arrested and in the next few days several thousand volunteers followed them to jail. At the same time the ANC grew to 100,000 paid-up members. When riots broke out the government imprisoned and banned Mandela and deposed Luthuli as a chief. Although the Defiance Campaign attracted international attention few whites in South Africa supported the African struggle. Non-Europeans had to fight alone. A mark of their solidarity was the Congress of the People, held in 1955 at Kliptown, where three thousand representatives met to frame a freedom charter which proclaimed:

South Africa belongs to all who live in it, black and white, and no government can justly claim authority unless it is based on the will of the people. . . . Our people have been robbed of their birthright to land, liberty and peace by a form of government founded on injustice and inequality.

On the second day the police broke-up the meeting. In the following year, in a series of dawn raids, most of the leaders of the ANC, including Oliver Tambo, Walter Sisulu, Nelson Mandela and Albert Luthuli, were arrested. Along with one hundred and fifty others they were accused of being involved in an international communist conspiracy to overthrow the government. The famous Treason Trial dragged on for four years and eventually most of the accused were acquitted, but only after they had suffered the long strain of constant attendance at court.

The pass laws became the next target for the ANC. A new, more militant political party was also involved, the Pan-African Congress, led by Robert Sobukwe, a young university lecturer. It was planned that on a certain day Africans without their passes would present themselves at police stations and demand to be arrested. Some protesters were dispersed but at

Ex-chief Albert Luthuli being congratulated by the King of Norway after he had received the Nobel Prize for peace.

Sharpeville the police opened fire on the crowd, killing sixty-nine and wounding one hundred and seventy-eight. There was an international outcry and the ANC called for a day of mourning during which many Africans in the towns stayed away from work. The white government promptly declared a state of emergency, mobilized the army, declared Congress and the PAC unlawful organizations, and arrested their leaders.

By the end of 1960 the government had effectively crushed African nationalism. It was also starting on the next major development in *apartheid*, turning the rural African reserves into self-governing tribal home-lands, or Bantustans. The architect of apartheid was Dr Verwoerd, who became prime minister in 1958. Total separation of the races was not possible because South African industry and agriculture, the richest in the whole continent, depended upon a plentiful sup-ply of black labour. Under *apartheid*, said Dr Ver-woerd, all the Africans 'have their permanent homes in the Reserves and their entry into other areas is merely of a temporary nature and for economic reasons. In other words they are admitted as work seekers, not as settlers'.

After Sharpeville both the ANC and the PAC went underground. Mandela, only recently released from prison, became leader of a National Action Council which called for a three day stay-at-home as a protest against the government's refusal to listen to the African voice. A warrant was issued for his arrest and he became a political outlaw, travelling around the

country in disguise and gaining a reputation as the 'Black Pimpernel'. When several hundred thousand Africans risked their jobs and livelihoods to stay at home the government turned out its troops. To many Africans this was a milestone for it showed 'that fifty years of non-violence had brought the African people nothing but more and more repressive legislation, and fewer rights'. In the middle of 1961 Mandela and a number of other Africans, along with some whites and Asians, formed a secret militant organization called *Mkhonto we Sizwe* — 'Spear of the Nation'. MK, as it became known, planned to sabotage selected targets such as electricity transmission lines and adminis-trative buildings but to avoid harming anybody. A few days before the first act of sabotage, in December 1961, ex-chief Luthuli was presented with the Nobel Prize for Peace in Oslo. He still held strongly to his belief in 'non-violent passive resistance', because, as he said,

I am convinced that it is the only non-revolutionary, legiti-mate and humane way that could be used by people denied, as we are, effective constitutional means to further aspira-tions.

And Luthuli held to these ideals despite further ban-nings and harsh restrictions until his tragic accidental death in 1967.

While the bulk of Congress followed Luthuli's line of peaceful methods, Nelson Mandela chose a revolutionary path. Within a short time he was ar-rested and sentenced to five years' imprisonment for inciting people to stay at home and for leaving the country illegally. The controlled sabotage of MK led to individual acts of murder and the more extreme PAC formed a terrorist group called *Poqo* —meaning 'pure', or 'we go it alone' — which announced that white rule would be overthrown in 1963. Riots and more killings continued and the government repression became even harsher. African newspapers were closed down, white

The shooting at Sharpeville. Ian Berry, the photographer who took these pictures, later told what happened: 'People were shot in literally every direction from the police station . . . there were people running towards me and I kept on taking pictures as I lay in the grass. The people didn't take it seriously at first; they thought the police were firing blanks. Children were running towards me . . . some holding their jackets up over their heads, presumably to fend off the bullets.

A woman who was just running past me a few feet away was shot in the back and fell next to me.'

liberals were put under house arrest, and by a system of ninety-day detention people could be imprisoned in solitary confinement without trials.

On a winter's afternoon in July 1963 policemen concealed in a dry-cleaners' van descended on a farm at Rivonia, in the suburbs of Johannesburg, where they seized Walter Sisulu and other MK leaders. Along with Mandela, who was brought from prison for trial, the eight men were accused of treason. At his earlier trial, in 1962, Nelson Mandela had warned that 'government violence can do only one thing and that is to breed counter-violence'. He now openly admitted his part in organizing sabotage. From the dock he made this moving speech:

During my lifetime I have dedicated myself to this struggle of the African people. I have fought against white domination, and I have fought against black domination. I have cherished the ideal of a democratic and free society in which all persons live together in harmony and with equal opportunities. It is an ideal which I hope to live for and achieve. But if needs be, it is an ideal for which I am prepared to die.

Mandela and Sisulu were found guilty and sentenced to life imprisonment. Other opponents of the government fled the country. Today the repressive white regime still holds South Africa in a firm grip.

Population in South Africa, 1971

	millions	urban %
African	14·975	30
Coloured	2·036	71
Asian	0·633	87
Whites	3·779	88
Total	21·423	

African and coloured population increasing four times faster than whites.
Africaaners outnumber English-speaking whites.

Prison statistics in South Africa, 1969—70

850 people detained as political prisoners
2000 people arrested every day for pass offences
90,000 people in prison (63,000 Africans) on any one day

People taken to prison during year ending 30 June 1968

561,405	Africans
77,374	Coloureds
13,792	Whites
2,325	Asians
654,896	Total

119 people were executed, half the world's known judicial executions.

Only a few whites in South Africa have actively opposed the racialist policies of the government. Mrs Helen Joseph, a British-born social worker, seen here saluting some of her sympathizers, was banned under the Suppression of Communism Act. This meant she was confined to her home, not allowed to have visitors, attend public meetings or write articles, and had to report each day to the police.

Black Africa's attitude to South Africa

Since 1965 South Africa has been increasingly concerned with her security and her long-term economic prosperity. She has made greater efforts to break out of her African isolation and to gain diplomatic recognition from the independent black states to the north. Land-locked Malawi was the first to do this in 1969. Dr Banda, the President of Malawi, has said:

'I am not supporting *apartheid* in South Africa. . . . But my argument is this: boycotts, isolation, ostracism are no solution to this problem. The more you try to boycott and isolate South Africa the more South Africa thrives. My solution is getting to know each other, African leaders meeting white leaders.'

Many African states refuse to trade with or recognize South Africa, Rhodesia and the Portuguese in Angola and Mocambique. They also give aid to the African nationalist movements fighting against these 'hostile white minorities' in the south. The Lusaka Manifesto on Southern Africa, signed in 1969 by thirteen African states, declared:

'What we are working for is the right of self-determination for the people of those territories. . . . We have always preferred, and we still prefer, to achieve it without physical violence. We would prefer to negotiate rather than destroy, to talk rather than kill. . . . But when peaceful progress is blocked by the action of those at present in power in the states of Southern Africa, we have no choice but to give to the people of those territories all the support of which we are capable in their struggle against their oppressors.'

One of the African states most hostile to *apartheid* is Tanzania. Its President, Julius Nyerere, has said:

'If South Africa wishes for dialogue with Africans she can start talking to her own people first.'

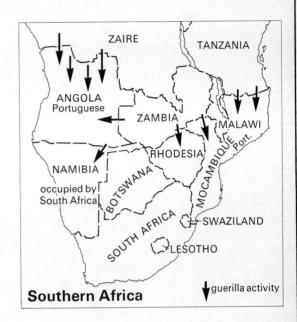

Southern Africa

guerilla activity

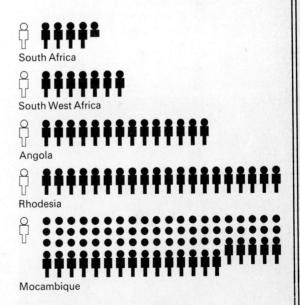

South Africa

South West Africa

Angola

Rhodesia

Mocambique

Ratios of whites to blacks

The laws of apartheid

1913 **Native Land Act** rights of 4 million Africans (78 per cent of population) restricted to 7·3 per cent of land in South Africa. The African awoke to find himself an outcast in the land of his birth.'

1936 **Native Trust and Land Act** land available for Africans increased to 13 per cent

Representation of Natives Act removed Cape Africans from common voting roll.

1945 **Native (Urban Areas) Consolidation Act** strengthened 1923 law and further restricted African movements to urban areas; Africans lived in locations or townships and were subject to curfew regulations.

1948 National Party became government with mandate for policy of *apartheid*.

1949 **Prohibition of Mixed Marriages Act** marriages between white and non-white made illegal.

1950 **Immorality Act** made sexual relations between white and non-white illegal.

Population Registration Act every person classified according to race as White, Bantu, Coloured, or Asiatic, and this shown in their identity card.

Suppression of Communism Act Communist Party outlawed and its members banned. Communism was widely defined to be any doctrine 'which aims at bringing about any political, industrial, social or economic change within the Union by the promotion of disturbances or disorder' or by 'the encouragement of feelings of hostility between the European and non-European races of the Union'. The Act has been used to suppress opponents of the government irrespective of their political beliefs.

Group Areas Act designated separate living areas, or homelands, for different racial groups to which people could be moved.

1952 **Natives (Abolition of Passes and Co-ordination of Documents) Act** all Africans compelled to carry a pass or reference book.

1953 **Reservation of Separate Amenities Act** enforced separate facilities for different races. The Act restricted non-white use of libraries, art galleries and public transport. Later extended to beaches, entrances to public buildings and so on.

A pass book.

The land of notices.

Public Safety Act government could declare a state of emergency and govern without Parlament.

Criminal Law Amendment Act made passive resistance to any law illegal.

Bantu Education Act separate schools for Africans and use of the vernacular languages. Extended to universities in 1959.

1956 **Industrial Conciliation Act** strikes by Africans were already illegal and now Africans could no longer form or belong to trade unions.

1959 **Promotion of Bantu Self-Government Act** ended indirect representation of Africans in Parliament. Eight separate African governments with limited powers and subject to the veto of Parliament were to be set up in the African homelands. Transkei was the first of these 'Bantustans' in 1963.

By two acts in 1956 and 1967 voting rights and indirect representation of coloured people were removed.

1960 **Unlawful Organizations Act** government banned the African National Congress and the Pan-African Congress.

1962– **General Law Amendment Acts** govern-
1964 ment took sweeping powers to prohibit meetings, ban, place under house arrest, and to detain people for repeated periods of ninety days without trial. Sabotage was made a treasonable offence and was defined to mean almost anything.

1965 **Criminal Procedure Act** state could detain people in solitary confinement for one hundred and eighty days as a means of forcing them to be state witnesses in criminal trials.

1967 **Terrorism Act** security police given wide powers of inquiry beyond control of courts or public opinion.

1968 **Prohibition of Improper Interference Act** made multi-racial political organizations illegal.

1969 **General Law Amendment Act** Bureau of State Security (BOSS) set up. Act also prevented a person from giving evidence even in his *own* defence if that evidence was not in the interest of the state.

1970 **Bantu Homeland Citizenship Act** all Africans formally made 'citizens' of one or other of the tribal homelands or proposed 'Bantustans'.

Left: Servants' quarters on top of a block of luxury flats. Black Servants are not allowed to live under the same roof as their white employers.

Little of South Africa's wealth reaches these school children.

Julius Nyerere
b. 1921

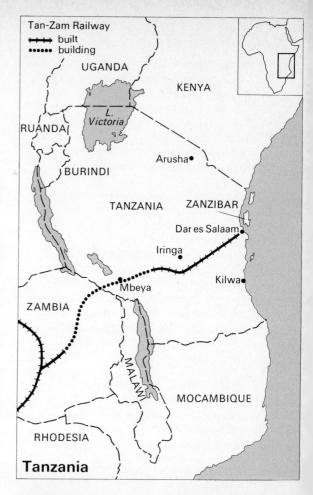

The 1200-mile-long Tanzania — Zambia Railway will tie the trade of the two countries more closely together.

Julius Nyerere was born in northern Tanganyika, the son of the chief of the small Zanaki tribe. When he was twelve years old he began his formal schooling in a Roman Catholic school and since then he has been a devout Christian. Nyerere has ability and determination and he worked hard. He became a teacher and then, in 1949, he went to Britain to study at Edinburgh University. There he gained an MA degree and learnt more about politics. On his return home Nyerere went back to teaching and also resumed his activities in the Tanganyika African Association (TAA) of which he became president.

The TAA had been formed in 1929 by a small group of educated Africans. It attempted to coordinate the activities of the various African welfare and improvement associations and also demanded that Africans be given 'a voice in the government'. The sense of nationalism increased after 1945, especially in the rural areas where protests were made against attempts by the colonial government to evict African farmers from their land. The TAA grew in strength and by 1954 representatives from all over the country met to turn it into a national political organization called the Tanganyika African National Union (TANU). The new party's slogan was *Uhuru na Umoja* —'Freedom and Unity'. At the United Nations Nyerere explained TANU's policy:

> Our main objective politically is the preparation of the people of Tanganyika for self-government and independence. . . . We mean to work towards self-government in a constitutional way.

TANU rapidly gained support throughout the country. This was partly due to good organization but Tanganyika also had several advantages over other African countries. First of all, although there were one hundred and twenty tribal and language groups most were small and unable to dominate political life or threaten national unity. Secondly, Tanganyika had a 'national' language, Swahili, a *lingua franca* which was understood right across the country so that TANU officials could travel from village to village talking to peasants and listening to their complaints. Thirdly, unlike neighbouring Kenya, there were few white settlers to resist African advancement, and finally, there was no large group of African businessmen who might fashion TANU's policies for their own interests.

During the 1950s the colonial government in

Tanganyika followed a policy known as multi-racialism. In order to protect the interests of the very small minority of Europeans and Asians who dominated the country's economy, the government insisted on equal representation for all three races in the advisory Legislative Council, although about 99 per cent of the population were Africans. As the leader of TANU, Nyerere agreed to serve on the Council but when it became obvious to him that the multi-racial policy was not going to be changed he resigned. By 1958, when the first elections for the Legislative Council were held, TANU had become a large party with about 200,000 members which was also supported by a few Europeans and Asians. When it won all the seats it contested, the colonial government, in particular the moderate-minded new governor, Sir Richard Turnbull, realized that the government could not maintain the system of racial representation or withhold independence much longer from Tanganyika. In the election of 1960 TANU dramatically swept the polls and Julius Nyerere became Chief Minister in the government. At the end of the following year the Union Jack was hauled down for the last time and replaced by the green, black and gold flag of independent Tanganyika. In the middle of the Uhuru celebrations Nyerere, a small spare man with a neat moustache and a light voice, warned his people that the more difficult task of 'nation building' was only just beginning:

It is essential we remember that what we have won is the right to work for ourselves, the right to design and build our own future. We have to build Tanganyika ourselves, primarily with our own resources and by our own efforts.

The unity of the country had to be strengthened, the three evils 'poverty, ignorance and disease' overcome, and the system of government inherited from colonial times adapted to Tanganyika's needs.

When Tanganyika became independent in 1961 TANU was in effect the only political party. There were

Most Tanzanians are farmers, and they are concerned with political questions in the same way as people in Europe or America are. Julius Nyerere speaking to Maasai cattle herders during the presidential election, 1963.

a few very small opposition groups but they had little support. For example, in the general election of 1960 TANU put up candidates in all seventy-one constituencies; fifty-eight were returned unopposed and therefore without anybody voting, and twelve seats were won outright. Thus in the National Assembly, or Parliament, TANU formed the government with seventy members and the opposition consisted of one lone man. It was obvious that the inherited British electoral system designed for a country with two major parties was unsuited to Tanganyika. Nyerere saw that the government and the party could become unrepresentative and undemocratic and that what was needed was a new system that would allow electors to vote regularly and change the government if they wished. Most people in the west think that a one-party state must mean a dictatorship. In Africa this may be so, as in Ghana under Nkrumah, but Nyerere has argued that the one party is logical in Africa because the vast majority of the population are peasants with similar economic and social problems. He has written:

Where that party is identified with the nation as a whole, the foundations of democracy are firmer than they can ever be where you have two or more parties, each representing only a section of the community.

In 1963 Tanganyika became a one-party state with TANU the only legal party. All elections, whether for Parliament, local government or party office, were to be contested by candidates drawn from TANU. The first test of these principles came in the parliamentary elections of 1965. A number of MPs, including several ministers, were defeated by relatively unknown local men because they had either lost touch with the ordinary people or appeared 'too arrogant, fat and self-satisfied in office'. The elections showed that even illiterate peasants were concerned with the everyday government of their country and also that a one-party state could be democratic.

Tanganyika (it became Tanzania in 1964) is a desperately poor country. Since independence the government has concentrated on developing the economy — building roads and schools, opening factories, irrigating the land, and helping farmers to improve their crops. All black African states have similar problems but they have attempted to solve them in different ways. Tanzania's way is through 'socialism and self-reliance'. President Nyerere has asked a very important question about the future of Tanzania: what kind of society are we trying to build? His answer is that

we want to create a socialist society which is based on three principles: equality and respect for human dignity; sharing of the resources which are produced by our efforts; work for everyone and exploitation by none.

Tanzania's socialism is called in Swahili *Ujamaa*, which means 'Familyhood'. It is based, claims Nyerere, on the way in which the communal life of the traditional African village was organized. The village worked together and 'if the tribe prospered, all the members of the tribe shared in its prosperity'. Similarly, in modern Tanzania the national wealth must be equally shared among the people and no one must be in a position to 'exploit his fellows'.

During colonial rule and the early years of independence a small number of Africans — businessmen, civil servants and party officials — had become relatively well off. They had good incomes, cars and comfortable houses and formed a privileged group — an elite. It is easy to understand why ordinary peasants began to think there were two classes of people, 'a lower class consisting of people who work for their living, and an upper class consisting of those who live on other people's labour'. Nyerere was determined to change this. In 1967 a TANU conference met at the small

16,000 Chinese and 30,000 Africans are building the Tan-Zam Railway which is now a year ahead of schedule. Due to open in 1976, the railway will give Zambia a new outlet for her copper exports

northern town of Arusha and decided how *Ujamaa* was to be maintained and applied. The Arusha Declaration outlined measures to prevent the growth of inequality and almost immediately ministers and party members were forbidden to have more than one income while large businesses and banks were nationalized. Like most African countries Tanzania had relied upon money from foreign countries, most of which had been used to develop industries in the towns so that frequently agriculture and the rural areas, where most of the people lived, had been neglected. Nyerere urged Tanzanians to rely on their own efforts, to work hard, and to produce more food and cash crops which could be exported to earn money.

This is the only road through which we can develop our country . . . and get more food and money for every Tanzanian.

The system of education also had to be changed. Children in primary schools had to be given a complete education, including learning agricultural skills, rather than studying for secondary schools to which few would have the opportunity to go. And those pupils who were fortunate to reach secondary schools and university were reminded by Nyerere that they had a responsibility 'to use their knowledge to help the development of this country'.

Under Nyerere's leadership Tanzania has followed a foreign policy of non-alignment, that is, it has refused to be tied either to the communist 'east' or the capitalist 'west'. When the World Bank failed to provide the money to build a railway across southern Tanzania to the Zambia copper belt Nyerere did not hesitate to accept China's offer of financial and technical assistance. Some people have suggested that Tanzania is in danger of being dominated by China, but it is important to remember that she has received more aid from western countries and that at the moment there are many more Europeans than Chinese living and working in the country.

Since it became independent Tanzania has been one of the most stable countries in a continent of political instability. There have been problems as is only to be expected in a developing country trying to bring about drastic economic progress and engineer social change — an army mutiny over pay, a treason trial, and the very great difficulties of the union with the authoritarian regime in Zanzibar. Julius Nyerere has been the national leader for nearly twenty years, preaching racial tolerance and earning his Swahili title of *Mwalimu* — 'teacher'. By keeping in close touch with ordinary Tanzanians and leading a simpler way of life than most African presidents he has voiced the needs and the hopes of his people.

The problems of independent Africa

In 1945 there were only four independent states in Africa — Ethiopia, Liberia, South Africa and Egypt, which was still occupied by British troops. By 1965 the number had increased to nearly forty. The new nations have in nearly all cases retained the old colonial frontiers, many of which are straight lines drawn in the late nineteenth century without regard to the African inhabitants. The frontier between Ghana and Togo, for example, divides the Ewe people, of whom there are about one million, into two almost equal groups, one in an English-speaking and the other in a French-speaking territory. Most African states south of the Sahara are faced with one or more problems that threaten their fragile national unity: different languages, tribal rivalries, religious differences and conflicting regional economic interests. Nigeria, one of the biggest countries in Africa and with the largest population — sixty-five million in 1970 — has four major tribal groups speaking distinct languages — the Hausa and Fulani in the north, the Ibo and Yoruba in the south, as well as many other smaller linguistic groups. Northern Nigeria is predominantly Muslim, more sparsely populated, economically less developed and consequently poorer than the south, which has a more advanced system of formal education and has been influenced by Christianity.

Africa is a developing area, part of the under-privileged, economically poor two-thirds of the world that suffers from poverty, ignorance and disease. Development is hindered by the unkind physical environment: the continent is large and communications difficult because of the terrain; there are large areas of arid and semi-arid country; rainfall is unevenly spread throughout the year and 90 per cent of Africa either has too much or too little rain at any one time; the soils are generally poor; mineral fuel resources such as coal and oil are scarce; and the majority of Africans in tropical regions suffer from the debilitating effects of one or more diseases such as malaria, bilharzia, yellow fever and sleeping sickness.

The economic poverty of Africa can be crudely compared to the relatively wealthy developed countries by the following examples:

In 1962 the Tanzanian Government's total revenue of £21 million was about equal to the sum spent each year on cleaning the streets of New York City.

In Nigeria there is one doctor to every forty thousand people while the United Kingdom has about one to every eight hundred people.

In the republic of Senegal only 5 per cent of the adult population can read; the figure for the United States is about 97 per cent.

The average annual income per head in Ethiopia is below £30; in Britain it is over £450.

Africa has what is sometimes called a 'colonial' type economy. Most African countries are dependent for much of their revenue on the export of a limited range of primary products such as cash crops and minerals to the developed parts of the world. For example, Senegal's main export is groundnuts, while 95 per cent of Zambia's total export earnings in 1969–70 came from copper. Nearly all roads and railways were built to ports to serve the export trade. World market prices for primary commodities are liable to fluctuate.

Africa has little manufacturing industry, few people with industrial or technical skills, and limited capital with which to finance the building of hospitals, roads, dams and factories. Machinery and consumer goods have to be imported from the developed countries which also lend finance for development. Thus although an African country may be politically independent its economy can still be controlled by foreign interests. Former President Nkrumah of Ghana called this *neo-colonialism*:

For those who practise it, it means power without responsibility and for those who suffer from it, it means exploitation without redress.

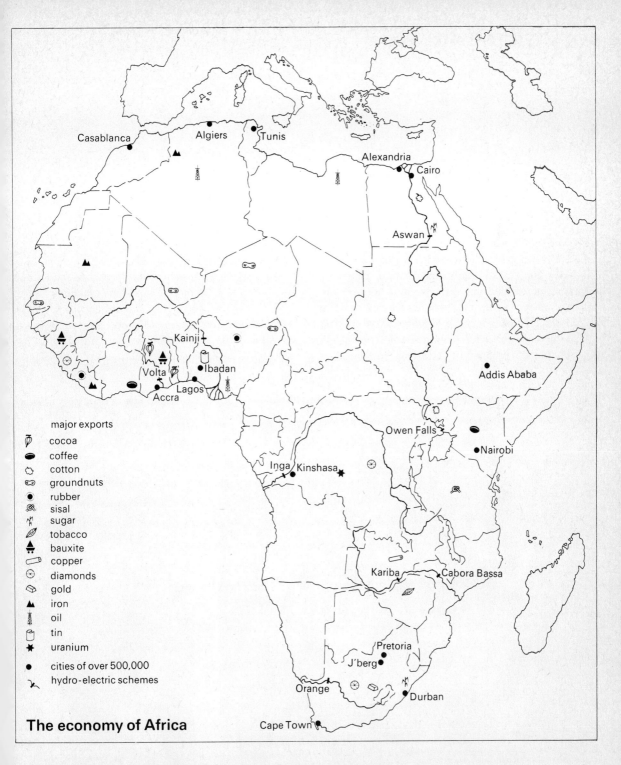

Casablanca
Algiers
Tunis
Alexandria
Cairo
Aswan
Kainji
Ibadan
Volta
Accra
Lagos
Addis Ababa
Owen Falls
Nairobi
Inga
Kinshasa
Kariba
Cabora Bassa
Pretoria
J'berg
Orange
Durban
Cape Town

major exports

- 🍈 cocoa
- coffee
- cotton
- groundnuts
- rubber
- sisal
- sugar
- tobacco
- bauxite
- copper
- diamonds
- gold
- iron
- oil
- tin
- uranium
- ● cities of over 500,000
- hydro-electric schemes

The economy of Africa

117

7 Africa's future?

The problem of the twentieth century is the problem of the colour line — the relation of the darker to the lighter races of men in Asia and Africa, in America and the islands of the sea.

These words were written over seventy years ago by William Du Bois, the great Afro-American champion. In some ways his prophecy was true. Almost any newspaper we pick up today has news about conflict between white and black — in South Africa, Rhodesia, Vietnam, the United States and Britain. However, perhaps the real division of the world is not over the colour of people's skin but between the rich and the poor, between those who have a high standard of living with access to health, education and comfort, and those who do not. Compared to the living standards of Europeans, Americans and Japanese most Africans are extremely poor; their lives are generally hard, frequently short, and with few material rewards. In all African countries there are a few comparatively wealthy people — those in government and business, and the white minorities in the south of the continent — and it is this wealth that millions of African peasants and workers wish to share and enjoy.

All African governments are trying to modernize their countries. In face of enormous economic, social and political problems they are attempting to create new nations from groups of people who in the past have had little sense of unity; more important, they are trying to develop their national economies and

African contrasts: Southern Sudan and Congo.

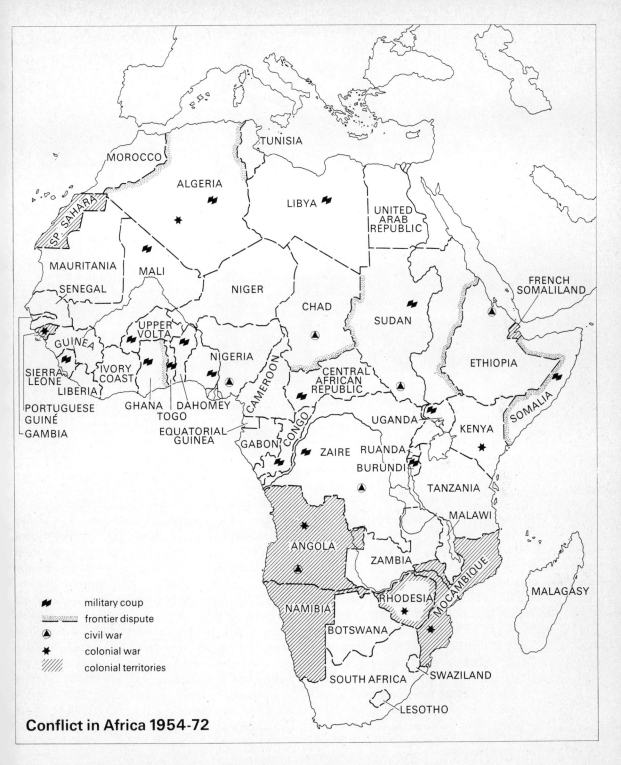

MOROCCO

TUNISIA

ALGERIA

LIBYA

UNITED ARAB REPUBLIC

SP. SAHARA

MAURITANIA

MALI

SENEGAL

NIGER

CHAD

SUDAN

FRENCH SOMALILAND

ETHIOPIA

GUINEA

UPPER VOLTA

NIGERIA

SIERRA LEONE

IVORY COAST

LIBERIA

GHANA

DAHOMEY

TOGO

CAMEROON

CENTRAL AFRICAN REPUBLIC

SOMALIA

PORTUGUESE GUINÉ

GAMBIA

EQUATORIAL GUINEA

GABON

CONGO

UGANDA

KENYA

ZAIRE

RUANDA

BURUNDI

TANZANIA

MALAWI

ANGOLA

ZAMBIA

NAMIBIA

RHODESIA

MOÇAMBIQUE

MALAGASY

BOTSWANA

SOUTH AFRICA

SWAZILAND

LESOTHO

	military coup
	frontier dispute
	civil war
	colonial war
	colonial territories

Conflict in Africa 1954-72

Africans in Rhodesia in 1972 gave an overwhelming 'No' to the British Government's attempt to settle the UDI dispute with the white minority regime. Rhodesia is not yet legally independent.

raise the living standards of the people. Is this possible? Can Africa ever be as prosperous as the developed countries of the world? Some people have argued that for technical reasons this cannot happen, that the world's resources of energy and raw materials are limited and therefore Africans cannot expect to reach the high level of the affluent world. Others put their faith in new technologies which they hope will provide fresh sources of power, materials and foodstuffs. But, even if this technological revolution did happen the world economy would probably still be dominated by the interests of the rich manufacturing countries. Therefore to make possible a more equal distribution of the world's wealth it may be necessary for radical changes to be made in the economic and social institutions of the rich nations.

Although African leaders want economic change for their countries many of them are also concerned that modernization should not lead to the destruction of the values and social stability in traditional family and communal life. Yet, inevitably, economic change brings social change. New roads, new factories and mines, and expanding towns mean that many Africans in search of a better life are confronted by a whole range of new social problems and economic frustrations. With so many problems and tensions it is not surprising that certain African countries suffer from sudden and violent changes of government. What is less noticed, however, is that many African states have had long periods of political stability and are relatively peaceful places.

The same cannot be said for the future of southern

African nationalist guerillas occupy a large part of the small Portuguese West African colony of Guiné. It is probably only a question of time before the Portuguese are forced to withdraw. Children training as guerillas in the forests.

Africa. For years political violence and economic exploitation have been the instruments by which the white minorities in South Africa, Rhodesia and the Portuguese colonies have ruled over large numbers of blacks. This explosive situation is not merely an internal affair but involves the future peace of Africa and, indeed, of the whole world.

How long will it be before the blacks are strong enough, either in numbers or economic strength, to challenge and change these regimes? It is probably only a matter of time before Portugal, the last colonial power in Africa, is driven out of Moçambique and Angola by the nationalist guerilla armies. Once this has happened the small group of white settlers in Rhodesia, already faced with a new vitalized African opposition, will be more vulnerable and less likely to survive.

South Africa, however, is a very different matter. Some observers forecast black bitterness boiling over into large-scale bloody violence, but it is difficult to see this happening while the comparatively large white minority retains effective control over a modern industrial state and a well-equipped military force. Political and social change in South Africa will probably be slow. It can only be brought about by whites and blacks inside the country, as blacks grow more confident of their own strength and as whites realize that they have created an authoritarian system of government which not only represses blacks but is increasingly destroying the rights of white people as well. The rest of the world, meanwhile, has a responsibility to add economic pressure to its moral condemnation of *apartheid* and racialism in southern Africa.

Further information

This list gives information about some books, places and things dealing with the study of Africa.

Bibliography

Books more suitable for reference purposes because of their inclusiveness and length are marked □. Books suitable for younger readers are marked ■, but most of them are suitable for adults too. Most of the books published since 1955 are still in print. Earlier books should be available in large libraries, and some may in any case be reprinted by the time you read this book.

Source books

Many of these are long, and written in an old-fashioned style, but they are invaluable because they contain detailed accounts and descriptions of Africa as it seemed to people at the time. Many of them are being reprinted but they are generally expensive. However, it is still possible to buy cheap second-hand copies of books written by British explorers. The most easily obtained sources are in anthologies.

Anthologies

Edgar Brookes (ed.), *Apartheid: A Documentary Study of Modern South Africa* (Routledge & Kegan Paul, 'World Studies' series, 1968). Speeches, Acts of Parliament, extracts, but unfortunately almost ignores the African presence.

□ Basil Davidson (ed.), *The African Past: Chronicles from Antiquity to Modern Times* (Longman, 1964; Penguin, 1966). Splendid and indispensable.

□ G. S. Freeman-Grenville (ed.), *The East African Coast* (Oxford University Press, 1962). Documents from the first to the nineteenth century.

■ Norah Latham (ed.), *The Heritage of West Africa* (Hulton, 1964). A selection covering the period from Herodotus to independence.

□ Colin Legum and John Drysdale (eds.), *Africa Contemporary Record: Annual Survey and Documents* (Africa Research, volumes for 1968–9, 1969–70, 1970–71). Valuable, up-to-date, detailed information.

■ Zoë Marsh (ed.), *East Africa through Contemporary Records* (Cambridge University Press, 1961), Mainly European sources up to the early twentieth century.

M. Perham and J. Simmons (eds.), *African Discovery* (Faber, 1942; new edition 1963). The best selection from the writings of British explorers.

Three anthologies covering the major English-speaking territories of West Africa are: Christopher Fyfe (ed.), *Sierra Leone Inheritance* (Oxford University Press, 1964); Freda Wolfson (ed.), *Pageant of Ghana* (Oxford University Press, 1958); and Thomas Hodgkin (ed.), *Nigerian Perspectives* (Oxford University Press, 1960).

T. Walter Wallbank (ed.), *Documents on Modern Africa* (Van Nostrand Anvil books, 1964). A selection since 1870.

Histories and biographies

■ John Addison, *Ancient Africa* (Rubert Hart-Davis, 'Young Historian's books' 1970). Clearly written account of Africa before the coming of the Europeans.

□ J. F. Ade Ajayi and Michael Crowder (eds.), *History of West Africa*, vol. 1 (Longman, 1971), a detailed and comprehensive history up to 1800. A second volume will appear in 1973.

□ J. F. Ade Ajayi and Ian Espie (eds.), *A Thousand Years of West African History* (Ibadan University Press and Nelson, 1965). See next item.

□ J. C. Anene and Godfrey Brown (eds.), *Africa in the Nineteenth and Twentieth Centuries* (Ibadan University Press and Nelson, 1966). Both contain a series of essays written by scholars and intended for teachers and upper secondary-school pupils. Excellent value.

Mary Benson, *The Struggle for a Birthright* (Penguin, 1966; first published as *The African Patriots*, Faber, 1965) recounts the history of the African National Congress in South Africa.

■ Mary Benson, *Chief Albert Luthuli of South Africa* (Oxford, 'Three Crowns' series, 1963). A brief biography.

David Birmingham, *The Portuguese Conquest of Angola* (Oxford University Press for the Institute of Race Relations, 1965). Well-written and stimulating short study.

■ A. Boahen, *Topics in West African History* (Longman 'Forum' series, 1966).

Paul Bohannan, *African Outline* (Penguin, 1964) is by far the best brief interdisciplinary introduction to the African continent.

E. W. Bovill, *The Golden Trade of the Moors* (Oxford University Press, 1958 —with an introduction by Robin Hallett; originally published as *Caravans of the Old Sahara*, 1933), looks at the kingdoms of the Western Sudan and the trans-Saharan trade.

■ A. Boyd and P. Van Rensburg, *An Atlas of African Affairs*, (Methuen, new edition 1965). A clear treatment of recent events.

H. A. C. Cairns, *Prelude to Imperialism; British Reactions to Central African Society, 1840—90* (Routledge & Kegan Paul, 1965). Fascinating and valuable study of the activities and attitudes of white men.

Philip Curtin, *The Image of Africa* (Macmillan, 1964), examines British ideas about West Africa from the late eighteenth century to the mid-nineteenth century. Wide-ranging and extremely well written.

□ Michael Crowder, *The Story of Nigeria* (Faber, 1962) is the best history. Basil Davidson, *Black Mother* (Gollancz, 1961). A study of the slave trade, with a distinctive interpretation about the effects on African society.

□ Basil Davidson, *Africa: History of a Continent* (Weidenfeld & Nicolson, 1966). Marvellous collection of photographs.

Basil Davidson, *Which Way Africa?* (Penguin, 1964, revised edition, 1967). Full of provocative ideas about Africa's search for a new society.

■ Basil Davidson, *History of West Africa 1000—1800* (Longman, 'The Growth of African Civilization' series, 1965) is intended for school-certificate level in African secondary schools. Excellent text, good illustrations, clear maps and cheaply priced, as are the other books in the series: ■ Basil Davidson, *East and Central Africa to the late Nineteenth Century* (1967); ■ J. B. Webster and A. Boahen, *The Revolutionary Years: West Africa since 1800* (1967); ■ J. D. Omer-Cooper, E. A. Ayendele, R. J. Gavin and A. E. Afigbo, *The Making of Modern Africa*. Vol. 1 (1968) covers the nineteenth century to Partition, and Vol. 2 (1971) covers the story to the present.

René Dumont, *False Start in Africa* (Deutsch, 1966; Sphere, 1968). Now a classic. A brilliant critical analysis of the economic problems of the French-speaking West African states.

Olaudah Equiano, *The Interesting Narrative of the Life of Olaudah Equiano* (1789), There is an abridged edition by

■ Paul Edwards, *Equiano's Travels* (Heinemann 'African Writers' series, 1967) of this life story of an Ibo slave.

□ J. D. Fage, *A History of West Africa: An Introductory Survey* (Cambridge University Press, 1969; and substantially revised, fourth edition of *An Introduction to the History of West Africa*, 1955). Clearly written and up to date. Ideal book for fourth-year secondary pupils and above.

□ J. D. Fage, *An Atlas of African History* (Edward Arnold, 1958). An essential book.

J. D. Fage (ed.) *Africa discovers her past*, (Oxford University Press, 1970), twelve short essays examining methods and sources used in studying Africa's past.

Frantz Fanon, *The Wretched of the Earth* (MacGibbon & Kee, 1965; Penguin, 1967). The classic of the revolutionary struggle against colonialism.

□ Paul Fordham, *The Geography of African Affairs* (Penguin, 1965; revised edition, 1968). A first-class introduction.

James L. Gibbs (ed.), *Peoples of Africa* (Holt, Rinehart & Winston, 1965). Essays by anthropologists on fifteen sub-saharan cultures.

□ Robin Hallett, *Africa to 1875* University of Michigan Press, 1970). Extremely well written and with an excellent bibliography. A second volume is to appear.

□ Robin Hallett, *The Penetration of Africa to 1815* (Routledge & Kegan Paul, 1965), looks at European enterprise and exploration. Splendidly written.

□ Robin Hallett, *People and Progress in West Africa: An Introduction to the Problems of Development* (Pergamon, 1966). Lucid.

□ John Hatch, *A History of Post-War Africa* (Deutsch, 1965).

■ John Hatch, *Africa: The Rebirth of Self-Rule* (Oxford University Press, 1967) deals with modern Africa. Best book for middle years of secondary school.

□ Alex Hepple, *South Africa: A Political and Economic History* (Praeger, 1966). A good outline history.

□ Thomas Hodgkin, *Nationalism in Colonial Africa* (Frederick Muller, 1956), is the best book on the subject.

■ Obaro Ikime (ed.), *African Historical Biographies* (Heinemann, 1972), a series of brief booklets on emminent Africans in the nineteenth century: Menelik of Ethiopia; Khama of Botswana; Nana of the Niger Delta; Moshweshwe of Lesotho; Obaseki of Benin.

J. M. Kariuki, *'Mau Mau' Detainee* (Oxford University Press, 1963; Penguin, 1964). Disturbing account by an African detained by the British during the Kenya emergency.

Kenneth Kaunda, *Zambia Shall be Free* (Heinemann, 'African Writers' series, 1963). Simply written, sincere autobiography of Zambia's president.

V. Kiernan, *The Lords of Human Kind* (Weidenfeld & Nicolson, 1969; Penguin, 1972) is a fascinating and highly readable examination of how white men viewed non-European peoples during the imperial age.

■ David Killingray, *Samori Touré: Warrior King* (Hulton 'Round the World Histories' series, 1973) is a brief simply told story suitable for younger reader.

Colin Legum, *Congo Disaster* (Penguin, 1961), a mixture of first-class journalism and history.

□ Colin Legum (ed.), *Africa Handbook* (Blond, 1961; revised edition Penguin, 1969). Indispensible.

Nehemiah Levtzion, *Ancient Ghana and Mali*, (Metheun, 1973) draws on oral tradition, Arabic and European sources.

Roy Lewis and Yvonne Fox, *The British in Africa* (Weidenfeld & Nicolson, 1971), has some very good illustrations.

□ P. C. Lloyd, *Africa in Social Change* (Penguin, 1967).

Comprehensive and penetrating analysis of the changing social, political and economic structure of West Africa. Good bibliography.

Albert Luthuli, *Let My People Go* (Collins, 1962; Fontana, 1963). Clearly written autobiography.

☐ Robert Lystad (ed.), *The African World: A Survey of Social Research* (Praeger, 1965). Valuable and detailed summaries of research in major disciplines.

Donald R. Morris, *The Washing of the Spears* (Cape, 1966; Sphere, 1968). Lengthy but excitingly written account of the Zulu nation and the war of 1879.

Nelson Mandela, *No Easy Walk to Freedom* (Heinemann, 1965; 'African Writers' series, 1972), includes his major articles and speeches edited with biographical information by Ruth First.

Philip Mason, *The Birth of a Dilemma: The Conquest and Settlement of Rhodesia* (Oxford University Press, 1958). Well written and compassionate.

Govan Mbeki, *The Peasants' Revolt* (Penguin, 1964). African view of South Africa's policy of *apartheid*.

☐ Daniel McCall, *Africa in Time Perspective* (Boston and Ghana University Press, 1964), is an immensely stimulating account of how history can be reconstructed from unwritten sources.

■ Elizabeth M. McClelland, *The Kingdom of Benin in the Sixteenth Century* (Oxford University Press 'Cities and Societies' series, 1971). Clearly written and illustrated.

Alan Moorehead, *The Blue Nile* (Hamish Hamilton, 1962; large illustrated edition 1971; Four Square Books, 1969) and *The White Nile* (Hamish Hamilton, 1960; Penguin, 1966) are both brilliantly told stories about the exploration of the Nile valley.

Kwame Nkrumah, *Ghana: An Autobiography* (Nelson, 1959).

D. T. Niane, *Sundiata: An Epic of Old Mali* (Longman, 'Forum' series, 1965). Vivid story based on oral tradition about the founder of the Empire of Mali.

Julius Nyerere, *Essays on Socialism* (Oxford University Press, 1968), includes some of the basic documents on recent economic and political developments in Tanzania.

☐ B. A. Ogot and J. A. Kiernan, *Zamani: A Survey of East African History* (East African Publishing House and Longman of Kenya, 1968). Excellent collection of essays, drawing on recent research.

☐ Roland Oliver, *The Missionary Factor in East Africa* (Longman, 1952).

☐ Roland Oliver and J. D. Fage, *A Short History of Africa* (Penguin, 1962). The best short introduction to Africa's past.

☐ Roland Oliver (ed.), *The Dawn of African History* (Oxford University Press, 1961) is a collection of brief talks on African achievements before the coming of Europeans. Another volume, in a similar format, is ☐ Roland Oliver (ed.), *The Middle Age*

of African History (Oxford University Press, 1967) which deals with the period up to the early nineteenth century. Both are useful introductions.

☐ Roland Oliver and Anthony Atmore, *Africa since 1800* (Cambridge University Press, 1967). A scholarly outline history of the whole continent. Excellent maps.

James Pope-Hennessey, *Sins of the Fathers: The Atlantic Slave Traders, 1441–1807* (Weidenfeld & Nicolson, 1967; Sphere, 1970). Superbly told.

Terence Ranger (ed.), *Aspects of Central African History* (Heinemann, 1968). Useful essays mainly based on recent research.

R. Robinson & J. Gallagher, *Africa and the Victorians* (Macmillan, 1961). Suggests that the British role in the 'scramble for Africa' was principally motivated by strategic considerations.

Walter Rodney, *How Europe underdeveloped Africa* (Bogle-L'Ouverture Publications, 1972), a very readable Marxist interpretation of why Africa's economy is like it is today.

Edward Roux, *Time Longer than Rope* (Wisconsin University Press, 1948, 1964), deals with African political and trade-union reaction to white rule in South Africa.

☐ Stanlake Samkange, *Origins of Rhodesia* (Heinemann, 1968). Ndebele relations with Whites.

☐ Ronald Segal (ed.), *African Profiles* (Penguin, 1962; revised 1963). Biographies of African leaders. Useful but needs bringing up to date.

George Shepperson and Thomas Price, *Independent African: John Chilembwe and the Nyasaland Rising of 1915* (Edinburgh University Press, 1963). Detailed, gripping, long, but extremely readable.

Margaret Shinnie, *Ancient African Kingdoms* (Edward Arnold, 1965). Well written and well illustrated.

Ndabaningi Sithole, *African Nationalism* (Oxford University Press, 1959; revised edition, 1969). Very readable because it is simple and amusing.

Roger Summers, *Zimbabwe: A Rhodesian Mystery* (Nelson, 1965), is an account of recent archaeological research.

Harry Thuku, *An Autobiography* (Oxford University Press, 1970), is the story of the veteran Kenyan nationalist.

☐ Immanuel Wallerstein, *Africa: The Politics of Independence* (Knopf, Vintage Books, 1961). An excellent brief interpretation of the history of Africa. A good book to start with.

Immanuel Wallerstein, *Africa the Politics of Unity* Vintage Books, 1972) looks at events since independence.

☐ James Walvin, *The Black Presence: A Documentary History of the Negro in England* (Orbach & Chambers, 1971).

■ G. S. Were and D. A. Wilson, *East Africa through a Thousand Years* (Evans, 1968), is an excellent survey up to the present day. Well illustrated.

☐ Richard West, *Back to Africa* (Cape, 1970). Mainly a history of Sierra Leone and Liberia. Extremely well written.

■ Barry Williams, *Modern Africa* (Longman, 'Modern Times' series, 1970). Covers the twentieth century. Clearly written. Illustrated.

■ A. J. Wills, *The Story of Africa*, 2 vols. (University of London Press, 1968, 1969). Concerned with the people of Africa. Well written and with good illustrations.

Robin Winks (ed.), *British Imperialism: Gold, God and Glory* (Holt, Rinehart & Winston, 'European Problem Studies' series, 1963), contains a good selection of sources.

☐ Monica Wilson and Leonard Thompson, *History of South Africa*, 2 vols. (Oxford University Press, 1969, 1971). Detailed and scholarly.

Novels

In the last few years a large number of novels have been written by Africans. Many of these are published in paperback editions in the Heinemann 'African Writers' series, and by Fontana. The authors come from all over Africa and their writing varies considerably in quality.

Peter Abrahams, *Mine Boy* (Faber, 1946; Heinemann 'African Writers' series, 1963), is about a young African boy from the country who comes to work in Johannesburg and is plunged into the turmoil of urban slum life.

Chinua Achebe, *Things Fall Apart* (Heinemann, 1958; 'African Writers' series, 1962), is a beautifully balanced novel about the effects of early European penetration on village life in Eastern Nigeria. Another novel by Chinua Achebe, *No Longer at Ease* (Heinemann, 1960; 'African Writers' series, 1963), describes the attempts of a young Nigerian graduate to reconcile the interests of his job in the urban society of Lagos and the expectations of his family and village home.

Camara Laye, *The African Child* (Collins, 1955; Fontana, 1959), is a beautifully written autobiographical novel about a child growing up in French-speaking West Africa.

James Ngugi, *The River Between.* (Heinemann, 'African Writers' series, 1965), tells the tragic story of a young man who ties to steer a middle course between the white man, his religion and education, and the pride and traditions of the Gikuyu.

Ferdinand Oyono, *Houseboy* (Heinemann 'African Writers' series, 1966), a tragic but amusing book written in the form of a diary kept by Toundi, the Cameroonian servant of the local white Commandant.

Alan Paton, *Cry the Beloved Country* (Cape, 1949; Penguin, 1967), a book by a white South African which looks at the social problem of South Africa through the eyes of a black minister.

Stanlake Samkange, *On Trial for My Country* (Heinemann, 1966; 'African Writers' series, 1967). A historical novel describing in graphic terms how the white man seized Rhodesia from the Ndebele.

Other authors to look out for are Cyprian Ekwensi, Ezekiel Mphalele, Wole Soyinka, Nadine Gordimer, Amos Tutuola and Doris Lessing. Two useful anthologies are O. R. Dathorne and W. Feuser, *Africa in Prose* (Penguin, 1969), a collection of writings covering the last hundred years; and Ezekiel Mphalele, *African Writing Today* (Penguin, 1967).

Gerald Moore and Ulli Beier have edited a small collection of poems, *Modern Poetry from Africa* (Penguin, 1963). A brief, but helpful introduction to African literature is Gerald Moore's *Seven African Writers* (Oxford 'Three Crowns' series, 1962).

Magazines and journals

Two journals that include comment on current events in Africa, and which are suitable for use with senior pupils in secondary school, are the monthly *World Today* (Oxford University Press, for the Royal Institute of International Affairs); and *Third World* (formerly *Venture*), published ten times a year by the Fabian Society, 11 Dartmouth Street, London SW 1.

Africa is an illustrated monthly news magazine produced in London.

Tarikh (Longman, for Historical Society of Nigeria) is a bi-annual journal of African history for schools, colleges and graduates. Each issue usually deals with a theme and articles are written by scholars who draw on recent research. Past issues have been on 'Modernizers in Africa', 'Christianity in Modern Africa', 'The Peoples of Uganda in the Nineteenth Century'. Excellent.

Journal of African History (Cambridge University Press) an academic quarterly concerned with recent research, includes review articles and book reviews. Other journals to look for are the *Journal of Modern African Studies* (Cambridge University Press), and *African Affairs* (Oxford University Press), both of which are published quarterly. *Africa Report* is published nine times a year by The African-American Institute, in New York, and contains articles on politics, economics, art and music.

The Africa Bureau, 48 Grafton Street, London W1P 5LB, produces the bi-monthly *African Digest* of current news about Africa. It also produces 'Fact Sheets' covering the problems of Southern Africa and the areas of occupied by the portuguese.

Visual materials and services

The Extra-Mural Division of the School of Oriental and African Studies, University of London, Malet Street, London WC 1, provides advice and information for teachers who wish to incorporate aspects of African and Asian studies into the curriculum.

The Commonwealth Institute, Kensington High Street, London W 8, has permanent exhibition galleries and a well-stocked lending library open to teachers and student teachers. It operates a comprehensive loan service of slides, film strips, tapes and study material which is posted *free* to schools anywhere in the United Kingdom. It is especially good on social and cultural aspects of the Commonwealth countries in Africa.

Voluntary Committee for Overseas Aid and Development, 25 Wilton Street, London SW 1, published *The Development Puzzle*, a source book for teachers containing information on books and audio-visual materials for use in teaching about aid and development.

The Africa Bureau, 48 Grafton Street, London W1, produces a monthly *African Digest* and of news, 'Fact Sheets' about current problems in Africa.

The Africa Centre, 38 King Street, London WC 1, runs a social centre, a restaurant that serves African food, and organizes courses, conferences and lectures on a variety of topics. A splendid place with a bit of an African atmosphere.

Museums

The *British Museum* Department of Ethnography. Museum of Mankind is at 6 Burlington Gardens, London W1, where a small part of the museum's African materials are well displayed in air-conditioned comfort. Excellent booklets and postcards can be bought at reasonable prices. The museum also sells replica Benin bronzes and Asante gold weights, which are expensive.

The *Horniman Museum*, London Road, Forest Hill, London SE 23, has an ethnographic collection. Lectures for children and a Saturday Club are organized by the Schools Officer

At the *Wilberforce Museum*, High Street, Hull, there is a display of material on the trans-Atlantic slave trade and British abolitionist movement.

Further details about museums and their services can be obtained from the *Museums Association*, 87 Charlotte Street, London W1.

Index

Acknowledgements

page
6   Victoria and Albert Museum
8   Jean-Dominique Lajoux
10   British Museum
13   British Museum, photo by R. B. Fleming
15   Mansell Collection/Bibliothèque National, Paris
16   British Museum
17   British Museum, photos by John Freeman and R. B. Fleming
21   Royal Commonwealth Society, photo by John Webb
22   British Museum/British Museum photo by John Freeman
23   British Museum
26   Tanzania Information Services
27   Royal Commonwealth Society, photo by John Webb
28   Paul Popper
29   Aerofilm
30   United Society for the Propagation of the Gospel, photo by John Webb
31   Radio Times Hulton Picture Library/Kingston-upon-Hull Museum
34   Diana Phillips
35   Mansell Collection
37   Lord Harlech/Radio Times Hulton Picture Library
39   Royal Geographical Society, photo by John Freeman
40   Kingston-Upon-Hull Museum
42–3 National Maritime Museum
45   British Museum, photo by John Freeman
46   United Society for the Propagation of the Gospel, photo by John Webb
47   Historical Picture Services, Chicago
50   National Portrait Galley/British Museum, photo by John Freeman
52   Royal Geographical Society, photo by John Freeman/Livingstone Memorial Museum
53   Mansell Collection
54   Mansell Collection/London Electrotype Agency
55   Mansell Collection
57   United Society for the Propagation of the Gospel, photo by John Webb
58   United Society for the Propagation of the Gospel, photo by John Webb
59   British Museum/United Society for the Propagation of the Gospel, photo by John Webb
60   British Museum, photo by John Freeman

61   Historical Picture Service, Chicago
63   Historical Picture Service, Chicago
64   Foreign and Commonwealth Office Library, photo by Chris Barker
65   National Army Museum
67   United Society for the Propagation of the Gospel, photo by John Webb
69   Royal Commonwealth Society, photo by John Webb/London Electrotype Agency
73   London Electrotype Agency
74   National Army Museum/Foreign and Commonwealth Office Library, photo by Chris Barker
75   National Army Museum
77   London Electrotype Agency/Horniman Museum
81   Royal Commonwealth Society, photos by John Webb
83   Mansell Collection
86   London Electrotype Agency
87   London Electrotype Agency
88   Afrique Photo
90   Paul Popper
92   M. D. McCann
93   Associated Press
94   Associated Press/Keystone Press Agency
95   Camera Press/Keystone Press Agency
97   Associated Press/Camera Press
99   United Press International
100   Paul Popper
101   Paul Popper
102   National Army Museum
103   John Hillelson Agency
105   Associated Press
106   Associated Press
107   Camera Press/Keystone Press Agency
108   Associated Press
110   Camera Press/John Hillelson Agency
111   John Hillelson Agency
113   Camera Press
115   Camera Press
118   John Hillelson Agency/Afrique Photo
120   Camera Press
121   John Hillelson Agency

Penguin Education Illustration Department, 7, 11, 14, 19, 24, 2?
33, 51, 70/71, 79, 82, 91, 100, 103, 109, 117, 119.